Canon EOS Rebel T4i/650D:
From
Snapshots to
Great Shots

Jeff Revell

Peachpit
Press

Canon EOS Rebel T4i / 650D: From Snapshots to Great Shots
Jeff Revell

Peachpit Press
www.peachpit.com

To report errors, please send a note to errata@peachpit.com
Peachpit Press is a division of Pearson Education.

Project Editor: Valerie Witte
Production Editor: Lisa Brazieal
Copyeditor: Scout Festa
Proofreader: Patricia Pane
Composition: WolfsonDesign
Indexer: Valerie Haynes Perry
Cover Image: Jeff Revell
Cover Design: Aren Straiger
Interior Design: Riezebos Holzbaur Design Group
Back Cover Author Photo: Scott Kelby

ISBN-13: 978-0-321-88691-0
ISBN-10:   0-321-88691-7

9 8 7 6 5 4 3 2 1

Printed and bound in the United States of America

DEDICATION

For all the great folks at Peachpit for putting up with my special brand of insanity—you guys are great!

Contents

Introduction

Walk into any bookseller and you will see countless books on the subject of photography. Look a little further and you will locate the camera-specific books. It is this divide between the camera-specific and instructional photography books that inspired me to write this book. I was seeing a lot of books that were just sort of missing the mark—especially when it came to combining actual photographic instruction with the use of a specific brand and model of camera. So with that, I set about to write this book on the Canon T4i, not as a rehash of the owner's manual but as a resource to teach photography with the wonderful technology present in the T4i. I have put together a short Q&A to help you get a better understanding of just what it is that you can expect from this book.

Q: IS EVERY CAMERA FEATURE GOING TO BE COVERED?

A: Nope, just the ones I felt you need to know about in order to start taking great photos. Believe it or not, you already own a great resource that covers every feature of your camera: the owner's manual. Writing a book that just repeats this information would have been a waste of my time and your money. What I did want to write about was how to harness certain camera features to the benefit of your photography. As you read through the book, you will also see callouts that point you to specific pages in your owner's manual that are related to the topic being discussed. For example, in Chapter 6 I discuss the use of the AE Lock feature, but there is more information available on this feature in the manual. I cover the function as it applies to our specific needs, but I also give you the page numbers in the manual so you can explore it even further.

Q: SO IF I ALREADY OWN THE MANUAL, WHY DO I NEED THIS BOOK?

A: The manual does a pretty good job of telling you how to use a feature or turn it on in the menus, but it doesn't necessarily tell you *why* and *when* you should use it. If you really want to improve your photography, you need to know the whys and whens to put all of those great camera features to use at the right time. To that extent, the manual just isn't going to cut it. It is, however, a great resource on the camera's features, and it is for that reason that I treat it like a companion to this book. You already own it, so why not get something of value from it?

Q: WHAT CAN I EXPECT TO LEARN FROM THIS BOOK?

A: Hopefully, you will learn how to take great photographs. My goal, and the reason the book is laid out the way it is, is to guide you through the basics of photography as they relate to different situations and scenarios. By using the features of your T4i and this book, you will learn about aperture, shutter speed, ISO, lens selection, depth of field, and many other photographic concepts. You will also find plenty of full-page photos that include captions, shooting data, and callouts so you can see how all of the photography fundamentals come together to make great images. All the while, you will be learning how your camera works and how to apply its functions and features to your photography.

Q: WHAT ARE THE ASSIGNMENTS ALL ABOUT?

A: At the end of most of the chapters, you will find shooting assignments, where I give you some suggestions as to how you can apply the lessons of the chapter to help reinforce everything you just learned. Let's face it—using the camera is much more fun than reading about it, so the assignments are a way of taking a little break after each chapter and having some fun.

Q: SHOULD I READ THE BOOK STRAIGHT THROUGH OR CAN I SKIP AROUND FROM CHAPTER TO CHAPTER?

A: Here's the easy answer: yes and no. No, because the first four chapters give you the basic information that you need to know about your camera. These are the building blocks for using the camera. After that, yes, you can move around the book as you see fit because the later chapters are written to stand on their own as guides to specific types of photography or shooting situations. You can bounce from portraits to shooting landscapes and then maybe to a little action photography. It's all about your needs and how you want to address them. Or, you can read it straight through. The choice is up to you.

Q: I DON'T SEE ANY CHAPTERS DEVOTED TO VIDEO.

A: I know that one of the reasons you bought the T4i was probably its ability to capture video. I have covered some basic video setup information in Chapter 2, but I really wanted the focus of this book to be the photographic capabilities and possibilities. Don't worry, though—read the next Q&A and I think you will be happy.

Q: IS THERE ANYTHING ELSE I SHOULD KNOW BEFORE GETTING STARTED?

A: In order to keep the book short and focused, I had to be selective about what I included in each chapter. The problem is that there is a little more information that might come in handy after you've gone through all the chapters. So as an added value for you, I have written two bonus chapters: "Pimp My Ride" and "T4i Video: Beyond the Basics." The first chapter is full of information on photo accessories that will assist you in making better photographs. In it, you will find my recommendation for things like filters, tripods, and much more. The second chapter will lead you through some video tips and techniques to make your T4i movies even better. To access the bonus chapters, just log in to or join Peachpit.com (it's free), then enter the book's ISBN. After you register the book, a link to the bonus chapters will be listed on your Account page under Registered Products.

Q: IS THAT IT?

A: One last thought before you dive into the first chapter. My goal in writing this book has been to give you a resource that you can turn to for creating great photographs with your Canon T4i. Take some time to learn the basics and then put them to use. Photography, like most things, takes time to master and requires practice. I have been a photographer for 30 years and I'm still learning. Always remember that it's not the camera that makes beautiful photographs—it's the person using it. Have fun, make mistakes, and then learn from them. In no time, I'm sure you will transition from a person who takes snapshots to a photographer who makes great shots.

1

ISO 100
5 sec.
f/22
30mm lens

The T4i Top Ten List

TEN TIPS TO MAKE YOUR SHOOTING MORE PRODUCTIVE RIGHT OUT OF THE BOX

Getting a new camera is a pretty exciting thing; at least it always is for me. It's hard not to be tempted into throwing the battery in the camera, slapping on the lens, and snapping away. What I really should be doing is sitting down with my instruction manual to learn how to use all of the camera features, but what fun is that? After all, we all know that instruction manuals are for propping up that short leg on the family room table, right?

Of course, this behavior always leads me to frustration in the end—there are always issues that would have been easily addressed had I known about them before I started shooting. Maybe if I had a Top Ten list of things to know, I could be more productive without having to spend countless hours with the manual. So this is where we begin.

The following list will get you up and running without suffering many of the "gotchas" that come from not being at least somewhat familiar with your new camera. So let's take a look at the top ten things you should know before you start taking pictures with your Canon T4i.

CAMERA FRONT

A Remote Control Sensor
B Main Dial
C Shutter Release Button
D Red-Eye Reduction/Self-Timer Lamp

E EF Lens Align Mark
F EF-S Lens Align Mark
G Lens Release
H Depth of Field Preview

CAMERA BACK

A Menu Button
B INFO Button
C Rear LCD
D Dioptric Adjustment
E Live View/Record Button
F AE/AF Lock/Focus/Reduce Image

G Focus Point Selection/Enlarge Image
H Aperture/Exposure Compensation
I Speaker
J Quick Control
K White Balance/Up Cross Key
L Set

M Autofocus Selection/Right Cross Key
N Drive Mode Selection/Left Cross Key
O Picture Style/Down Cross Key
P Card Busy Lamp
Q Trash (Delete)
R Image Review

CAMERA TOP

A Pop-Up Flash
B Microphone
C ISO
D Shutter Release
E Main Dial
F On/Off/Movie Record
G Mode Dial
H Speedlite Hot Shoe

1. CHARGE YOUR BATTERY

I know that this will be one of the hardest things for you to do because you really want to start shooting, but a little patience will pay off later.

When you first open your camera and slide the battery into the battery slot, you will be pleased to find that there is probably juice in the battery and you can start shooting right away. Resist the temptation, and instead get out the battery charger and give that power cell a full charge. Not only will this give you more time to shoot later on, but it will also start the battery off on the right foot. No matter what claims the manufacturers make about battery life and battery memory, I always find I get better life and performance when I charge my batteries fully and then use them right down to the point where they have nothing left to give. To check your battery's level, insert it into the camera, turn on the camera, and look for the battery indicator on the rear LCD. You might have to press the shutter release button to wake up the camera. This will activate the rear LCD display and allow you to see the battery-level indicator, located in the lower-left portion of the display panel (**Figure 1.1**).

FIGURE 1.1
The LCD screen shows how much charge is left on your battery.

KEEPING A BACKUP BATTERY

If I were to suggest just one accessory that you should buy for your camera, it would probably be a second battery. Nothing stinks more than being out in the field and having your camera die. Keeping a fully charged battery in your bag will give you the confidence that you can keep on shooting without fail. Not only will this extend your shooting time, but alternating between batteries will help lengthen their lives. No matter what the manufacturers say, batteries do have a life, and using them half as much will only lengthen their usefulness.

2. TURN OFF THE RELEASE SHUTTER WITHOUT CARD SETTING

If you really want to ruin your day, try shooting for a couple of hours only to find that you didn't put a memory card in your camera and thus didn't save any of the pictures you took. This was always a concern with film shooters, and it hasn't gone away with digital SLRs. You see, camera manufacturers want to give prospective buyers a way to test out the camera without having to keep a memory card in it, so they came up with a setting called Release Shutter Without Card. When your camera is set up in this mode, it will act and shoot just as it would when you have a memory card inserted. It will even display your shot on the rear LCD display. Unfortunately, this is where most photographers get fooled into thinking they are saving their images. If they were to look at the LCD, they would see that Canon was nice enough to overlay a message on the display that clearly says No Card. This is nice, but if you are shooting without looking at the display, you could easily be fooled.

Unfortunately, there is no visual clue within the viewfinder to alert you to this No Card status. So here is the simple solution.

TURNING OFF THE RELEASE SHUTTER WITHOUT CARD SETTING

1. Turn the camera on.
2. Press the Menu button on the back of the camera to bring up the menu list.
3. Use the Main dial to select the far-left menu tab.
4. Now use the Cross keys to scroll down to the Release shutter without card option, and press the Set button (**A**).
5. Use the Cross keys to select the Disable option, and then press the Set button once again (**B**).
6. Press the Menu button again to return to shooting mode.

A

B

Now when you try to take a photo without a memory card inserted in the camera, you will see the word *Card* flashing in the bottom left of your viewfinder. This is your clue that you need to insert your memory card before the camera will fire. The rear display will also display a large No Card message if you activate the shutter button (**Figure 1.2**). We will have an in-depth discussion on memory cards and proper formatting in Chapter 2.

FIGURE 1.2

After deactivating the Release Shutter Without Card setting, you will see a "No card in camera" message if you have not inserted a memory card.

3. SET YOUR JPEG IMAGE QUALITY

Your new T4i has a number of image-quality settings to choose from, and you can adjust them according to your needs. Most people shoot with the JPEG option because it allows them to capture a large number of photos on their memory cards. The problem is that unless you understand how JPEG works, you might be degrading the quality of your images without realizing it.

The JPEG (Joint Photographic Experts Group) format has been around since about 1994 and was developed as a method of reducing large file sizes while retaining the original image information. (Technically, JPEG isn't even a file format—it's a mathematical equation for reducing image file sizes—but to keep things simple, we'll just refer to it as a file format.) The problem with JPEG is that, in order to reduce file size, it has to throw away some of the information. This is referred to as "lossy compression." This is important to understand, because while you can fit more images on your memory card by choosing a lower-quality JPEG setting, you will also be reducing the quality of your image. This effect becomes more apparent as you enlarge your pictures.

The JPEG file format also has one other characteristic: to apply the compression to the image before final storage on your memory card, the camera has to apply all of the image processing first. Image processing involves such factors as sharpening, color adjustment, contrast adjustment, noise reduction, and so on. Many photographers now prefer to use the RAW file format to get greater control over the image processing. We will take a closer look at this in Chapter 2, but for now let's just make sure that we are using the best-quality JPEG possible.

The T4i has eight quality settings for the JPEG format. There are two settings each for the Large, Medium, and Small settings. The two settings represent more or less image compression based on your choice. The Large, Medium, and Small settings determine the actual physical size of your image in pixels. There are also two additional settings (Small 2 and Small 3) that are even smaller in physical size than Small 1 but do not have compression options.

Manual Callout

For a chart that shows the image quality settings with the number of possible shots for each setting, turn to page 87 in your user manual.

Let's work with the highest-quality setting possible. After all, our goal is to make big, beautiful photographs, so why start the process with a lower-quality image?

SETTING THE IMAGE QUALITY

1. Press the Menu button on the back of the camera to bring up the menu list.
2. Use the Main dial to select the far-left menu tab.
3. At the top of this menu tab, locate the Image quality option (**A**).
4. Press the Set button to bring up the options screen.
5. Use the left/right Cross keys to select the first L (this will render an 18-megapixel image with a dimension of 5184 pixels by 3456 pixels) (**B**).
6. Press the Set button to lock in this change.

A

B

4. TURN OFF THE AUTO ISO SETTING

The ISO setting in your camera allows you to choose the level of sensitivity of the camera sensor to light. The ability to change this sensitivity is one of the biggest advantages to using a digital camera. In the days of film cameras, you *had* to choose the ISO by film type. This meant that if you wanted to shoot in lower light, you had to replace the film in the camera with one that had a higher ISO. So not only did you have to carry different types of film, but you also had to remove one roll from the camera to replace it with another, even if you hadn't used up the current roll. Now all we have to do is go to the menu and select the appropriate ISO.

Having this flexibility is a powerful option, but just as with the Quality setting, the ISO setting has a direct bearing on the quality of the final image. The higher the ISO, the more digital noise the image will contain. Since our goal is to produce high-quality photographs, it is important that we get control over all of the camera controls and bend them to our will. When you turn your camera on for the first time, the ISO will be set to Auto. This means that the camera is determining how much light is available and will choose what it believes is the correct ISO setting. Since you want to use the lowest ISO possible, you will need to turn this setting off and manually select the appropriate ISO.

Which ISO you choose depends on your level of available or ambient light. For sunny days or very bright scenes, use a low ISO such as 100 or 200. As the level of light is reduced, raise the ISO level. Cloudy days or indoor scenes might require you to use ISO 400. Low-light scenes, such as when you are shooting at night, will mean you need to bump up that ISO to 1600 or higher. The thing to remember is to shoot with the lowest setting possible for maximum quality. Later, we will cover some other specifics of exposure so that you know just how and why to raise your ISO.

SETTING THE ISO

1. Activate the camera by lightly pressing the shutter release button.

2. Press the ISO button on the top of the camera.

3. Use the Main dial to select an ISO between 100 and 6400.

4. Lightly press the shutter release button or press the ISO button again to lock in your change.

NOISE

Noise is the enemy of digital photography, but it has nothing to do with the loudness of your camera operation. It is a term that refers to the electronic artifacts that appear as speckles in your image. They generally appear in darker shadow areas and are a result of the camera trying to amplify the signal to produce visible information. The more the image needs to be amplified—e.g., raising the sensitivity through higher ISOs—the greater the amount of noise there will be.

SET YOUR ISO ON THE FLY

By following the steps above, you can change the ISO without taking your eye from the viewfinder. When you press the ISO button, all of the camera settings in the viewfinder will disappear, leaving just the ISO information. Once you press the Shutter Release button, your new ISO setting will be displayed along with the regular shooting data. This will get easier to do as you become more familiar with the camera buttons.

5. SET YOUR FOCUS POINT AND MODE

The Canon focusing system is legendary for its speed and accuracy. The Artificial Intelligence (AI) focus modes will give you a ton of flexibility in your shooting. There is, however, one small problem that is inherent with any focusing system. No matter how intelligent it is, the camera is looking at all of the subjects in the scene and determining which is closest to the camera. It then uses this information to determine where the proper focus point should be. It has no way of knowing what your main emphasis is, so it is using a "best guess" system. To eliminate this factor, you should set the camera to single-point focusing so that you can ensure that you are focusing on the most important feature in the scene.

The camera has nine separate focus points to choose from. They are arranged in a diamond pattern, with eight points around the outside of the diamond and one in the center. To start things off, you should select the focus point in the middle. Once you have become more familiar with the focus system, you can experiment with the other points, as well as with the automatic point selection.

You should also change the focus mode to One Shot so that you can focus on your subject and then recompose your shot while holding that point of focus. This method will allow for better composition.

SETTING THE FOCUS POINT AND FOCUS MODE

1. To choose a single point of focus, wake the camera (if necessary) by lightly pressing the shutter release button.
2. Press the focus point selection button, located in the upper-right area of your camera back.
3. Now use the Cross keys or the Main dial to move the focus point to the center spot, as seen on the rear LCD display (you can also do this in the viewfinder by moving the red dot to the desired position) (**A**).
4. Lightly press the shutter release button once more to set your new focus point.
5. To set the focus mode, press the AF button, which doubles as the right Cross key.
6. Using the Cross keys or the Main dial, select the One Shot mode, then press the Set button (**B**).

FIGURE 1.3
Using the center single-focus point in One Shot mode allows you to focus on your subject in the center and then recompose your photograph for a better composition.

The camera is now ready for single focusing. You will hear a chirp when the camera has locked in and focused on the subject. To focus on your subject and then recompose your shot, just place the focus point in the viewfinder on your subject, depress the shutter release button halfway until the camera chirps, and without letting up on the shutter button, recompose your shot and then press the shutter button all the way down to make your exposure (**Figure 1.3**).

6. SET THE CORRECT WHITE BALANCE

White balance correction is the process of rendering accurate colors in your final image. Most people don't even notice that light has different color characteristics, because the human eye automatically adjusts to changes in color temperature—so quickly, in fact, that everything looks correct in a matter of milliseconds.

When color film ruled the world, photographers would select which film to use depending on what their light source was going to be. The most common film was balanced for daylight, but you could also buy film that was color balanced for tungsten light sources. Most other lighting situations had to be handled by using color filters over the lens. This process was necessary for the photographer's final image to show the correct color balance of a scene.

Your camera has the ability to perform this same process automatically, but you can also choose to override it and set it manually. Guess which method we are going to use? You are catching on fast! Once again, your photography should be all about maintaining control over everything that influences your final image.

Luckily, you don't need to have a deep understanding of color temperatures to control your camera's white balance. The choices are given to you in terms that are easy to relate to and that will make things pretty simple. Your white balance choices are:

- **Auto:** The default setting for your camera. It is also the setting used by all of the Basic modes (see Chapter 3).

- **Daylight:** Most often used for general daylight/sunlit shooting.

- **Shade:** Used when working in shaded areas that are still using sunlight as the dominant light source.

- **Cloudy:** The choice for overcast or very cloudy days. This and the Shade setting will eliminate the blue color cast from your images.

- **Tungsten:** Used for any occasion where you are using regular household-type bulbs for your light source. Tungsten is a very warm light source and will result in a yellow/orange cast if you don't correct for it.

- **White Fluorescent:** Used to get rid of the green-blue cast that can result from using regular fluorescent lights as your dominant light source. Some fluorescent lights are actually balanced for daylight, which would allow you to use the Daylight white balance setting.

- **Flash:** Used whenever you're using the built-in flash or a flash on the hot shoe. You should select this white balance to adjust for the slightly cooler light that comes from using a flash. (The hot shoe is the small bracket located on the top of your camera; it rests just above the eyepiece. This bracket is used for attaching a more powerful flash to the camera; see Chapter 8 and the bonus chapter "Pimp My Ride.")

- **Custom:** Indicates that you are using a customized white balance that is adjusted for a particular light source. If you know what the color temperature of your light source is, you can manually create a white balance setting that is specifically for that light source.

Your camera has two different "zones" of shooting modes to choose from: Basic and Creative. They are located on the Mode dial. All of the Basic modes, which are identifiable by small icons, are automatic in nature and do not allow for much, if any, customization. The Creative modes, identified by letter symbols, allow for much more control by the photographer (**Figure 1.4**).

FIGURE 1.4
The camera's shooting modes are divided into the Basic zone and the Creative zone.

SETTING THE WHITE BALANCE

1. After turning on or waking the camera, select one of the shooting modes in the Creative zone, such as P (you can't set the white balance when using the Basic modes).

2. Press the WB button on the back of the camera to bring up the White balance menu. It is the top button on the Cross keys.

3. Use the left/right Cross keys to select the proper white balance for your shooting situation.

4. Press the Set button to lock in your selection.

5. Check the camera display to ensure that the proper white balance is selected.

WHITE BALANCE AND THE TEMPERATURE OF COLOR

When you select white balances in your camera, you will notice that underneath several of the choices is a number—e.g., 5200K, 7000K, or 3200K. These numbers refer to the Kelvin temperature of the colors in the visible spectrum. The visible spectrum is the range of light that the human eye can see (think of a rainbow or the color bands that come out of a spectrum). The visible spectrum of light has been placed into a scale called the Kelvin temperature scale, which identifies the thermodynamic temperature of a given color of light. Put simply, reds and yellows are "warm," and greens and blues are "cool." Even more confusing can be the actual temperature ratings. Warm temperatures are typically lower on the Kelvin scale, ranging from 3000 degrees to 5000 degrees, while cool temperatures run from 5500 degrees to around 10000 degrees. Take a look at this list for an example of Kelvin temperature properties.

KELVIN TEMPERATURE PROPERTIES

Flames	1700K–1900K	Daylight	5000K
Incandescent bulb	2800K–3300K	Camera flash	5500K
White fluorescent	4000K	Overcast sky	6000K
Moonlight	4000K	Open shade	7000K

The most important thing to remember here is how the color temperature of light will affect the look of your images. If something is "warm," it will look reddish-yellow, and if something is "cool," it will have a bluish cast.

7. ADJUST THE VIEWFINDER DIOPTER

If you wear glasses or your eyes are just getting older, you might have trouble looking through the viewfinder. Actually, you will be able to see through the viewfinder,
but what you see might not look like it is in crisp focus. This may not be a huge
problem when you are using autofocus, but if you are trying to manually focus your
lens, you will find that your images look a bit soft. To remedy this, use the dioptric
adjustment knob (located to the right of the viewfinder) to adjust things for your
vision. There is no "correct" setting for this adjustment, so you will have to dial it in
yourself. It's really easy if you know this little trick.

ADJUSTING THE DIOPTER

1. Remove your lens and point your camera
   at a light-colored wall or surface.

2. Place your index finger on the dioptric
   adjustment knob and look through the
   viewfinder (if you normally wear glasses,
   you should have them on).

3. Rotate the wheel until the focus points in
   the viewfinder look sharp.

4. That's it. Just replace your lens and start shooting with a clearer view.

If you have tried adjusting the diopter and still can't seem to get it right, you may
want to consider purchasing a dioptric lens to replace the standard viewfinder lens.
They can be found on the Canon website in the accessories section for the T4i.

8. TURN OFF THE TOUCHSCREEN

One of the great new features of the T4i is the touchscreen, which lets you interact
with the camera settings and menus with a touch of your finger. With a simple tap
of the finger on the rear LCD screen, you can quickly change a setting; with a swipe
across the screen, you can review your pictures. The only problem is that I sometimes
find that I have activated the screen when I didn't intend to. One way to combat this
is to flip the screen closed. While this method works, it is kind of inconvenient while
shooting because I have to flip it open every time I want to see an image that I shot.
An easier way to take care of this problem is to just turn off the touch control in the
camera menu.

TURNING OFF TOUCH CONTROL

1. Press the Menu button and navigate to the third Set-up menu.

2. Highlight the Touch control option and press the Set button (**A**).

3. Change the option to Disable and press the Set button (**B**).

Now that the touchscreen is disabled, it will no longer activate accidentally. One thing that you might want to do is add this option to your custom menu so that you can quickly access it when you want to turn it back on. We will cover the My Menu feature in Chapter 10.

9. REVIEW YOUR SHOTS

One of the greatest features of digital cameras is their ability to give us instant feedback. By reviewing your images on the camera's LCD screen, you can instantly tell if you got your shot. This visual feedback allows you to make adjustments on the fly and make certain that you nailed the shot before moving on.

When you first press the shutter release button, your camera quickly processes your shot and then displays the image on the rear LCD display. The default duration setting for that display is only 2 seconds. Personally, I don't find this to be nearly enough time to take in all the visual feedback that I might want. Instead of using this "quick glance" method, change your display time to the Hold setting. This will keep the image on the display until you decide that you are ready to move on to your next shot. (Note that this option will drain your batteries a little faster than the default setting.)

CHANGING THE IMAGE REVIEW TIME SETTING

1. Press the Menu button and then use the Main dial to select the leftmost menu item.

2. Use the Cross keys to scroll down to Image review, and press the Set button (**A**).

3. Scroll down to Hold and then press the Set button once again (**B**).

4. Press the Menu button to leave the menus and continue shooting.

A

B

Now that you have the image display set, let's check out some of the other visual information that will help you when shooting.

There are four display modes, and each gives you a different amount of information. The default view (**Figure 1.5**) simply displays your image.

To get more visual feedback, press the INFO button, located to the left of the viewfinder. Press it once to see shutter speed, aperture, file name, and the image number that you are currently viewing ("7/22" would mean that you're looking at the seventh image of 22 total images) (**Figure 1.6**).

FIGURE 1.5
The default display mode on the T4i.

FIGURE 1.6
Press the INFO button once to see the second display option.

Pressing the INFO button a second time results in a huge amount of information being displayed along with the image. You will now be able to see the following items in your display: shutter speed, aperture, exposure compensation, file name, image thumbnail, histogram, shooting mode, ISO, white balance setting, picture style, quality setting, meter mode, size of the image in megabytes, color space, image number, date, and time (**Figure 1.7**).

FIGURE 1.7
This display mode offers you a ton of information at a glance.

A Image Number	G Shutter Speed	M Picture Style
B Quality Setting	H Aperture	N Color Space
C White Balance	I Exposure Compensation	O Time
D Shooting Mode	J File Name	P Date
E Meter Mode	K Histogram	Q Image Size
F Image Thumbnail	L ISO	

That's a huge amount of information on a 3-inch screen! You probably won't want to use this display option as your default review setting, but if you are trying to figure out what settings you used or want to review the histogram (see the sidebar "The Value of the Histogram" on pages 20–21), you now have all of this great information available.

The fourth display option allows you to view the regular image histogram, as well as a color histogram for your image. I prefer to use the standard histogram, but you may find the color histogram handy when checking to see if you were able to capture all of the information in your scene (**Figure 1.8**).

FIGURE 1.8
The fourth display option shows you a color histogram.

Both histogram modes show a thumbnail-sized version of your image. So while there is a lot of information concerning the camera settings, you get less visual feedback in terms of seeing the actual photo. You would probably be best served by selecting one of the first two display modes and using the histogram modes only when you need to review your shooting data.

The different display modes are activated by pressing the INFO button while an image is displayed on your LCD screen. That display mode will remain for all future images until you press the INFO button again. Also, pressing the shutter release or Menu button will result in closing the image display. To get your image back up on the LCD screen, simply press the blue Image Review button on the back of the camera.

DELETING IMAGES

Deleting or erasing images is a fairly simple process that is covered on pages 224–225 of your manual. To quickly get you on your way, simply press the Image Review button and find the picture that you want to delete. Then press the Trash button (beneath the Cross keys), use the right Cross key to select Erase, and press the Set button (**Figure 1.9**).

Caution: Once you have deleted an image, it is gone for good. Make sure you don't want it before you drop it in the trash.

FIGURE 1.9
Deleting images on the T4i is simple.

THE VALUE OF THE HISTOGRAM

Simply put, histograms are two-dimensional representations of your images in graph form. There are two different histograms that you should be concerned with: luminance and color. Luminance is referred to in your manual as "brightness" and is most valuable when evaluating your exposures. In **Figure 1.10**, you see what looks like a mountain range. The graph represents the entire tonal range that your camera can capture, from the whitest whites to the blackest blacks. The left side represents black, and the right side represents white. The heights of the peaks represent the number of pixels that contain those luminance levels (a tall peak in the middle means your image contains a large number of medium-bright pixels). Looking at an image, it can be hard to determine where all of the ranges of light and dark areas are and how much of each I have. If I look at the histogram, I can see that the largest peak of the graph is in the middle and trails off as it reaches the edges. In most cases, you would look for this type of histogram, indicating that you captured the entire range of tones, from dark to light, in your image. Knowing that is fine—but here is where the information really gets useful.

A histogram that has a spike or peak riding up the far left or right side of the graph means that you are clipping detail from your image. In essence, you are trying to record values that are either too dark or too light for your sensor to accurately record. This is usually an indication of over- or underexposure. It also means that you need to correct your exposure so that the important details will not record as solid black or white pixels (which is what happens when clipping occurs). There are times, however, when some clipping is acceptable. If you are photographing a scene where the sun will be in the frame, you can expect to get some clipping, because the sun is just too bright to hold any detail. Likewise, if you are shooting something that has true blacks in it—think coal in a mineshaft at midnight—there are most certainly going to be some true blacks with no detail in your shot. The main goal is to ensure that you aren't clipping any "important" visual

FIGURE 1.10

This is a typical histogram, where the dark-to-light tones run from left to right. The black-to-white gradient above the graph demonstrates where the tones lie on the graph and does not appear above your camera's histogram display.

information, and that is achieved by keeping an eye on your histogram. Take a look at **Figure 1.11**. The histogram displayed on the image shows a heavy skew toward the left, with no part of the mountain touching the right side. This is a good example of what an underexposed image histogram looks like. Compare that to **Figure 1.12**, the histogram for the same image correctly exposed. Notice that even though there are two distinct peaks on the graph, there is an even distribution across the entire histogram.

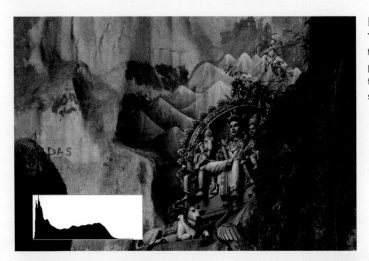

FIGURE 1.11
This image is about two stops underexposed. Notice that the histogram is skewed to the left.

FIGURE 1.12
This histogram reflects a correctly exposed image.

10. HOLD YOUR CAMERA FOR PROPER SHOOTING

Digital SLR cameras are made to favor the right-handed individual. The basics of properly holding the camera begin with grasping the camera body with the right hand. You will quickly find that most of the important camera controls are within easy reach of your thumb and forefinger. The next step is to create a stable base for your camera to rest on. This is accomplished by placing the camera body on the up-facing palm of your left hand (**Figure 1.13**). Now you can curl your fingers around the lens barrel to quickly zoom or manually focus the lens.

Now that you know where to put your hands, let's talk about what to do with the rest of your body parts. By using the underhand grip, your elbows will be drawn closer to your body. You should concentrate on pulling them in close to your body to stabilize your shooting position. You should also try to maintain proper upright posture. Leaning forward at the waist will begin to fatigue your back, neck, and arms. Nothing ruins a day of shooting like a sore back, so make sure you stand erect with your elbows in. Finally, place your left foot in front of your right foot, and face your subject in a slightly wide stance. By combining all of these aspects into your photography, you will give yourself the best chance of eliminating self-imposed camera shake (or hand shake) in your images, resulting in much sharper photographs.

FIGURE 1.13
The proper way to hold your camera to ensure sharp, blur-free images. (Photos by Alex Revell)

Chapter 1 Assignments

Let's begin our shooting assignments by setting up and using all of the elements of the Top Ten list. Even though I have yet to cover the Creative shooting modes, you should set your camera to the P (Program) mode. This will allow you to interact with the various settings and menus that have been covered thus far.

Basic camera setup

Charge your battery to 100% to get it started on a life of dependable service. Next, using your newfound knowledge, set up your camera to address the following: shooting without a card, image quality, and Auto ISO.

Selecting the proper white balance

Take your camera outside into a daylight environment and photograph the same scene using different white balance settings. Pay close attention to how each setting affects the overall color cast of your images. Next, move inside and repeat the exercise while shooting in a tungsten lighting environment. Finally, find a fluorescent light source and repeat once more.

Focusing with single point and One Shot

Change your camera setting so that you are focusing using the single-point focus mode. Try using all of the different focus points to see how they work in focusing your scene. Then set your focus mode to One Shot, and practice focusing on a subject and recomposing before actually taking the picture. Try doing this with subjects at varying distances.

Evaluating your pictures with the LCD display

Set up your image display properties, and then review some of your previous assignment images using the different display modes. Review your shooting information for each image, and take a look at the histograms to see how the content of your photo affects their shapes.

Get a grip: proper camera holding

This final assignment is something that you should practice every time you shoot: proper grip and stance for shooting with your camera. Use the described technique and then shoot a series of images. Try it with improper techniques to compare the stability of the grip and stance.

Share your results with the book's Flickr group!

Join the group here: flickr.com/groups/t4i650dfromsnapshotstogreatshots

2

ISO 640
1/2500 sec.
f/2.8
70mm lens

First Things First

A FEW THINGS TO KNOW AND DO BEFORE YOU BEGIN TAKING PICTURES

Now that we've covered the top ten tasks to get you up and shooting, we should probably take care of some other important details. You must become familiar with certain features of your camera before you can take full advantage of it. Additionally, we will take some steps to prepare the camera and memory card for use. So to get things moving, let's start off with something that you will definitely need before you can take a single picture: a memory card.

PORING OVER THE PICTURE

The Daylight white balance setting helped show off the warm early-morning light.

An aperture of f/6.3 blurs the background, but not so much that you can't identify the monument.

Living in the Washington, DC, area affords me a lot of great photographic opportunities, but one that I had never taken advantage of was the yearly blossoming of the cherry trees around the Tidal Basin. There is usually only a small window of opportunity for shooting them because of the weather and the short time they are on the trees. This year my timing was great, and everything came together just right for me to get some iconic shots of the blossoms.

ISO 100
1/500 sec.
f/6.3
40mm lens

The focus point was placed on the blossoms near the center before recomposing.

Because I was shooting in bright light, I could use a low ISO for maximum quality.

PORING OVER THE PICTURE

A very slow shutter speed was used to make the water look silky smooth.

The Landscape picture style really accentuates the greens and blues.

In order to get a slow shutter speed I had to use a small aperture, which also gave me a large depth of field.

One of the first chances I had for testing out the T4i was in the Columbia River Gorge, just outside Portland, Oregon. I was fortunate to have a beautiful day for shooting, and the beautiful waterfalls and lush greenery of the forests created the perfect location to put the camera through its paces. This particular waterfall presented some challenges because I had to shoot from a walkway that was very close. Instead of capturing the entire falls, I concentrated my efforts on this small section.

Using a low ISO setting also helped in getting a long exposure.

I placed the camera on a tripod to keep the scene free of camera shake.

ISO 100
1.3 sec.
f/22
35mm lens

CHOOSING THE RIGHT MEMORY CARD

Memory cards are the digital film that stores every shot you take until you move them to a computer. The cards come in all shapes and sizes, and they are critical for capturing all of your photos. It is important not to skimp when it comes to selecting your memory cards. The T4i uses Secure Digital (SD) memory cards (**Figure 2.1**).

FIGURE 2.1
Make sure you select an SD card that has enough capacity and speed to handle your photography needs.

If you have been using a point-and-shoot camera, you may already own an SD media card. Which brand of card you use is completely up to you, but here is some advice about choosing your memory card:

- Size matters, at least in memory cards. At 18 megapixels, the T4i will require a lot of storage space, especially if you shoot in the RAW or RAW+JPEG mode (more on this later in the chapter) or shoot HD video. You should definitely consider using a card with a storage capacity of at least 4 GB.

- Consider buying High Capacity (SDHC) cards. These cards are generally much faster, both when writing images to the card and when transferring them to your computer. If you are planning on using the Continuous mode (see Chapter 5) for capturing fast action, you can gain a boost in performance just by using an SDHC card with a Class rating of at least 6. The higher the Class rating, the faster the write speed. Having a fast card will also benefit your video capture by keeping the flow of video frames moving quickly to your card.

- Buy more than one card. If you have already purchased a memory card, consider getting another. It's a bad day when your card is almost full and you have to either erase shots or choose a lower-quality image format so that you can keep on shooting. With the cost of memory cards what it is, keeping a spare just makes good sense.

- To get the fastest memory possible, you could consider purchasing an SDXC memory card. Although they appear to be the same as SD and SDHC cards, they are made to new specifications that allow memory capacities above 32 GB. Your camera is SDXC compliant, but if you plan to share SDXC cards between devices such as your T4i and a video camera, make sure the other device is SDXC compatible too. SDXC cards will work only in SDXC devices. Also, you should format your SDXC card only in your camera.

Canon recommends a speed rating of at least Class 6 for shooting video. What you need to know is that all cards are not created equal. In the past, I have had issues with Class 6 cards that could not keep up with the demands of video recording and caused the camera to stop in the middle of a recording session. My recommendation is that, if you know you are going to be shooting video with your camera, you should use a Class 10 card to keep the pixels flowing.

FORMATTING YOUR MEMORY CARD

Now that you have your card, let's talk about formatting for a minute. When you purchase any new SD card, you can pop it into your camera and start shooting right away—and probably everything will work as it should. However, what you *should* do first is format the card in the camera. This process allows the camera to set up the card to record images from your camera. Just as a computer hard drive must be formatted, formatting your card ensures that it is properly initialized. The card may work in the camera without first being formatted, but chances of failure down the road are much higher.

As a general practice, I always format new cards or cards that have been used in different cameras. I also reformat cards after I have downloaded my images and want to start a new shooting session. Note that you should always format your card in the camera, not in your computer. Using the computer could render the card useless in your camera. You should also pay attention to the manufacturer's recommendations with respect to moisture, humidity, and proper handling procedures. It sounds a little cliché, but when it comes to protecting your images, every little bit helps.

Most people are under the impression that formatting the memory card is equivalent to erasing it. Not so. The truth is that when you format the card, all you are doing is changing the file management information on the card. Think of it as removing the table of contents from a book and replacing it with a blank page. All of the contents are still there, but you wouldn't know it by looking at the empty table of contents. The camera will see the card as completely empty, so you won't be losing any space, even if you have previously filled the card with images. Your camera will simply write the new image data over the previous data.

FORMATTING YOUR MEMORY CARD

1. Insert your memory card into the camera.

2. Press the Menu button and navigate to the first setup menu screen (the fifth from the right).

3. Press the down Cross key on the back of the camera to highlight the Format card option, and press Set (**A**).

4. The default selection for the Format card screen is Cancel, just in case you didn't really want to format the card (**B**). Press the right Cross key to highlight OK. The screen will warn you that you will lose any data by formatting your card, so make sure that you have saved any images that you want onto your computer or elsewhere before formatting.

5. Press the Set button to finalize the formatting of the card.

Note that when you perform the card formatting, you can select something called Low Level Format, which performs a much more intensive formatting of the card. During the process, the camera will format all of the recordable sectors on the card. This process takes much longer than a normal formatting and does not need to be performed every time you format. You only need to do this if you see a slowdown in card performance. To enable the Low Level Format option, simply follow the directions above but press the Trash button before starting the formatting process. This will put a check mark next to the Low Level Format option (**Figure 2.2**).

FIGURE 2.2
Press the Trash button to enable the Low Level Format option.

UPDATING THE T4i'S FIRMWARE

I know that you want to get shooting, but having the proper firmware can affect the way the camera operates. It can fix problems as well as improve operation, so you should probably take care of it sooner rather than later. Updating your camera's firmware is something that the manual completely omits, yet it can change the entire behavior of your camera operating system and functions. The firmware of your camera is the set of computer operating instructions that controls how your camera functions. Updating this firmware is a great way to not only fix little bugs but also gain access to new functionality. You will need to check out the information on the Canon firmware update page (www.canon.com/eos-d/) to review how a firmware update will affect your camera, but it is always a good idea to be working with the most up-to-date firmware version available.

CHECKING THE CAMERA'S CURRENT FIRMWARE VERSION NUMBER

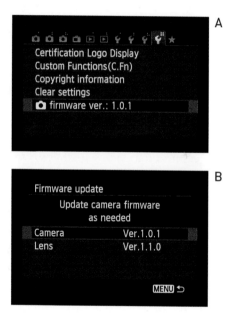

1. Rotate the Mode dial to select P (or any of the other modes in the Creative zone).

2. Press the Menu button to display the menu.

3. Turn the Main dial to get to the fourth camera setup menu (the second one from the right) and press Set (**A**).

4. Check the version numbers for the camera and lens (**B**). If these versions are not the latest ones listed on the Canon website, follow the steps in the next section to load the latest version.

At the time of this writing, the current version of the firmware for the T4i is 1.0.1 for the camera and 1.1.0 for the lens and no updates are available. Make sure you check the Canon webpage often for any updates, and then follow the directions on the following page for updating your camera.

UPDATING THE FIRMWARE USING THE EOS UTILITY PROGRAM

1. Download the firmware update file from the Canon website (**A**). (You can find the file by going to the Download Library section of the EOS camera site and entering the information about your camera.)

A

2. Download the Firmware Update file that matches your computer operating system (Windows or Macintosh).

3. Extract the downloaded firmware file as per your operating system (**B**).

B

4. Attach your camera to the computer via USB and turn the camera on (**C**).

5. Open the EOS Utility program and select the Camera settings/Remote shooting option (**D**). (This program was included on the CD in your camera box. You will need to install it prior to performing this operation.)

6. When the panel opens, click the Set-Up icon and then click the Firmware button at the bottom of the panel.

7. Click OK and then locate the extracted firmware file to begin the update (**E**).

8. Click Yes on the confirmation screen to begin the update. Note that the software will not allow you to continue the update unless the camera is plugged into the AC power adapter or the battery is fully charged.

UPDATING THE FIRMWARE IN-CAMERA

It is possible to update your camera's firmware by copying the Firmware Update file to your formatted SD card and updating in-camera instead of using the EOS Utility program. There is a complete set of instructions for using this method on the Firmware download webpage referred to in Step 1 above. You will still need a computer and a card reader to use this method, so make sure you follow the directions to the letter.

CLEANING THE SENSOR

Cleaning camera sensors used to be a nerve-racking process that required leaving the sensor exposed to scratching and even more dust. Now cleaning the sensor is pretty much an automatic function. Every time you turn the camera on and off, the sensor in the camera vibrates to remove any dust particles that might have landed on it.

There are three choices for cleaning in the camera setup menu: Auto Cleaning, Clean Now, and Clean Manually. By default, the camera is set to automatically clean the sensor every time you power on and off. You can disable this function, but it is best to leave it on.

The one cleaning function that you will need to use via this menu is the Clean Now feature. This should be done every time you remove the lens from the camera body. That is because removing or changing a lens will leave the camera body open and susceptible to dust sneaking into the body. If you never change lenses, you shouldn't have too many dust problems. But the more often you change lenses, the more chances you are giving dust to enter the body. It's for this reason that I have added the Clean Now function to the custom My Menu list (see Chapter 10).

Every now and then, there will just be a dust spot that is impervious to the shaking of the Auto Cleaning feature. This will require manual cleaning of the sensor. When you activate this feature, it will raise the camera mirror and give you access to the sensor so that you can use a blower or other cleaning device to remove the stubborn dust speck. The camera will need to be turned off after cleaning to allow the mirror to reset.

If you choose to manually clean your sensor, please use a device that has been made to clean sensors (not a cotton swab from your medicine cabinet). There are dozens of commercially available devices—such as brushes, swabs, and blowers—that will clean the sensor without damaging it. To keep the sensor clean, always store the camera with a body cap or lens attached.

The camera sensor is an electrically charged device. This means that when the camera is turned on, there is a current running through the sensor. This electric current can create static electricity, which will attract small dust particles to the sensor area. For this reason, it is always a good idea to turn off the camera prior to removing a lens. You should also consider having the lens mount facing down during lens removal so there is less opportunity for dust to fall into the inner workings of the camera.

USING THE CLEAN NOW FEATURE

1. Press the Menu button and use the Main dial to get to the third camera setup menu.

2. Use the down Cross key to highlight Sensor cleaning, and then press the Set button (**A**).

3. Use the Cross keys to select Clean now, and press the Set button again (**B**).

4. Press Set one more time to start the cleaning function.

5. To return to shooting mode, lightly press the shutter release button.

A

B

USING THE CLEAN MANUALLY FEATURE

1. Follow steps 1 and 2 above.

2. Use the right Cross key to select Clean manually, and press the Set button (**A**).

3. Use the right Cross key to select OK, and press the Set button again (**B**).

4. Remove your lens, carefully clean the sensor, and then replace the lens or put on the body cap.

5. Turn the camera off to reset.

A

B

USING THE RIGHT FORMAT: RAW VS. JPEG

When shooting with your T4i, you have a choice of image formats that your camera will use to store the pictures on the memory card. JPEG is probably the most familiar format to anyone who has been using a digital camera. I touched on this topic briefly in Chapter 1, so you already have a little background on what JPEG and RAW files are.

There is nothing wrong with JPEG if you are taking casual shots. JPEG files are ready to use, right out of the camera. Why go through the process of adjusting RAW images of the kids opening presents when you are just going to email them to Grandma? Also, for journalists and sports photographers who are shooting nine frames per second and need to transmit their images across the wire—again, JPEG is just fine. So what is wrong with JPEG? Absolutely nothing—unless you care about having complete creative control over all of your image data (as opposed to what a compression algorithm thinks is important).

As I mentioned in Chapter 1, JPEG is not actually an image format. It is a compression standard, and compression is where things can go bad. When your camera is set to JPEG—whether it is set to High or Low compression—you are telling the camera to process the image however it sees fit and then throw away enough image data to make it shrink into a smaller space. In doing so, you give up subtle image details that you will never get back in post-processing. That is an awfully simplified statement, but it's still fairly accurate.

SO WHAT DOES RAW HAVE TO OFFER?

First and foremost, RAW images are not compressed. (Some cameras offer a compressed RAW format, but it is lossless compression, which means there is no loss of actual image data.) Note that RAW image files will require you to perform post-processing on your photographs. This is not only necessary—it is the reason that most photographers use it.

RAW images have a greater dynamic range than JPEG-processed images. This means that you can recover image detail in the highlights and shadows that just aren't available in JPEG-processed images.

There is more color information in a RAW image because it is a 14-bit image, which means it contains more color information than a JPEG, which is almost always an 8-bit image. More color information means more to work with and smoother changes between tones—kind of like the difference between performing surgery with a scalpel as opposed to a butcher's knife. They'll both get the job done, but one will do less damage.

Regarding sharpening, a RAW image offers more control because you are the one who is applying the sharpening according to the effect you want to achieve. Once again, JPEG processing applies a standard amount of sharpening that you cannot change after the fact. Once it is done, it's done.

Finally, and most importantly, a RAW file is your negative. No matter what you do to it, you won't change it unless you save your file in a different format. This means that you can come back to that RAW file later and try different processing settings to achieve differing results and never harm the original image. By comparison, if you make a change to your JPEG and accidentally save the file, guess what? You have a new original file, and you will never get back to that first image. That alone should make you sit up and take notice.

ADVICE FOR NEW RAW SHOOTERS

Don't give up on shooting RAW just because it means more work. Hey, if it takes up more space on your card, buy bigger cards or more smaller ones. Will it take more time to download your images? Yes, but good things come to those who wait. Don't worry about needing to purchase expensive software to work with your RAW files; you already own a program that will allow you to work with your RAW files. Canon's Digital Photo Professional software comes bundled in the box with your camera and gives you the ability to work directly on the RAW files and then output the enhanced results.

My recommendation is that you shoot in JPEG mode while you are using this book. This will allow you to quickly review your images and study the effects of future lessons. Once you have become comfortable with all of the camera features, you should switch to shooting in RAW mode so that you can start gaining more creative control over your image processing. After all, you took the photograph—shouldn't you be the one to decide how it looks in the end?

IMAGE RESOLUTION

When discussing digital cameras, image resolution is often used to describe pixel resolution, or the number of pixels used to make an image. This can be displayed as a dimension, such as 5184 x 3456. This is the physical number of pixels in width and height of the image sensor. Resolution can also be referred to in megapixels (MP), such as 18 MP. This number represents the number of total pixels on the sensor and is commonly used to describe the amount of image data that a digital camera can capture.

SELECTING RAW + JPEG

Your camera has the added benefit of being able to write two files for each picture you take: one in RAW and one in JPEG. This can be useful if you need a quick version to email but want a higher-quality version for more advanced processing.

It should be noted that using both formats requires more space on the memory card. I recommend that you use only one format or the other unless you have a specific need to shoot both.

SELECTING YOUR IMAGE QUALITY SETTING

1. Press the Menu button, and use the Main dial to select the first shooting menu tab.

2. Use the Cross keys to highlight the Image quality setting, and press the Set button to enter the settings page (**A**).

3. Use the left/right Cross keys to change the quality setting (**B**).

4. Press the Set button to lock in your changes.

A

B

LENSES AND FOCAL LENGTHS

If you ask most photographers what they believe to be their most critical piece of photographic equipment, they would undoubtedly tell you that it is their lens. The technology and engineering that goes into your camera is a marvel, but it isn't worth a darn if it can't get the light from the outside world onto the sensor. The T4i, as a digital single lens reflex (DSLR) camera, uses the lens for a multitude of tasks, from focusing on a subject, to metering a scene, to delivering and focusing the light onto the camera sensor. The lens is also responsible for the amount of the scene that will be captured (the frame). With all of this riding on the lens, let's take a more in-depth look at the camera's eye on the world.

Lenses are composed of optical glass that is both concave and convex in shape. The alignment of the glass elements is designed to focus the light coming in from the front of the lens onto the camera sensor. The amount of light that enters the camera is also controlled by the lens, the size of the glass elements, and the aperture mechanism within the lens housing. The quality of the glass used in the lens will also have a direct effect on how well the lens can resolve details and the contrast of the scene (the ability to deliver great highlights and shadows). Most lenses now routinely include things like the autofocus motor and, in some cases, an image-stabilization mechanism.

There is one other aspect of the camera lens that is often the first consideration of the photographer: lens focal length, which determines the angle of view delivered through the lens. Lenses are typically divided into three or four groups, depending on the field of view they cover.

Wide-angle lenses cover a field of view from around 110 degrees to about 60 degrees (**Figure 2.3**). There is also a tendency to get some distortion in your image when using extremely wide-angle lenses. This will be apparent toward the outer edges of the frame. As for which lenses would be considered wide angle, anything 30mm or smaller could be considered wide.

ISO 100
1/200 sec.
f/13
18mm lens

FIGURE 2.3
The 18mm lens setting provides a wide view of the scene but little detail of distant objects.

Wide-angle lenses can display a large depth of field, which allows you to keep the foreground and background in sharp focus. This makes them very useful for landscape photography. They also work well in tight spaces, such as indoors, where there isn't much elbow room available (**Figure 2.4**). They can also be handy for large group shots but, due to the amount of distortion, not so great for close-up portrait work.

FIGURE 2.4
When shooting in tight spaces where you want to capture a large subject, a nice wide-angle lens helps capture more of the scene.

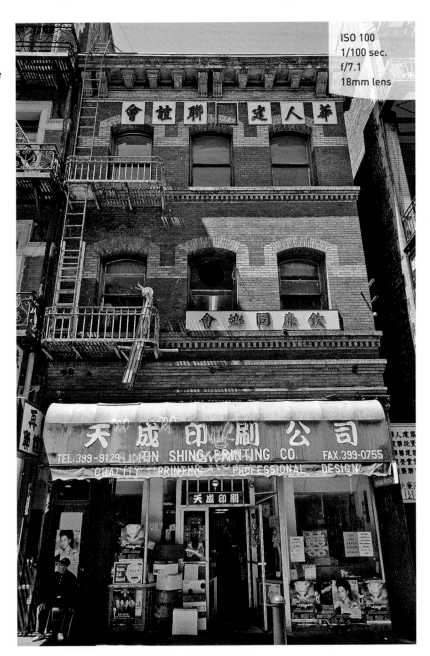

ISO 100
1/100 sec.
f/7.1
18mm lens

A *normal* lens has a field of view that is about 45 degrees and delivers approximately the same view as the human eye (not in angle of view but in size and perspective of subjects). The perspective is very natural, and there is little distortion in objects. The normal lens for full-frame and 35mm cameras is the 50mm lens, but for the T4i it is more in the neighborhood of a 35mm lens (**Figure 2.5**).

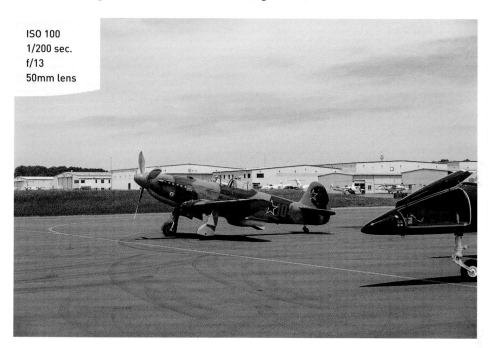

ISO 100
1/200 sec.
f/13
50mm lens

FIGURE 2.5
Long considered the "normal" lens for 35mm photography, the 50mm focal length can be considered somewhat of a telephoto lens on the T4i because it has the same angle of view and magnification as an 80mm lens on a 35mm camera body.

Normal focal length lenses are useful for photographing people, architecture, and most other general photographic subjects. They have very little distortion and offer a moderate range of depth of field (**Figure 2.6**).

Most longer focal length lenses are referred to as *telephoto* lenses. They can range in length from 100mm up to 800mm or longer and have a field of view that is about 35 degrees or smaller. These lenses have the ability to greatly magnify the scene, allowing you to capture details of distant objects, but the angle of view is greatly reduced (**Figure 2.7**). You will also find that you can achieve a much narrower depth of field. They also demonstrate something called distance compression, which means they make objects at different distances appear to be much closer together than they really are.

Telephoto lenses are most useful for sports photography or any application where you just need to get closer to your subject (**Figure 2.8**). They can have a compressing effect—making objects look closer together than they actually are—and a very narrow depth of field when shot at their widest apertures.

FIGURE 2.6
The normal lens worked well in this image by providing enough coverage to capture the cherry blossoms while keeping the monument large in the background.

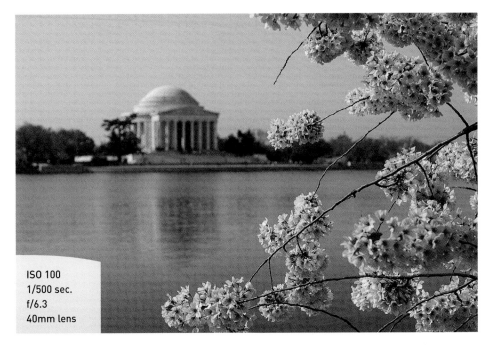

ISO 100
1/500 sec.
f/6.3
40mm lens

FIGURE 2.7
The telephoto lens allowed me to capture close-up detail of the plane without having to get physically closer.

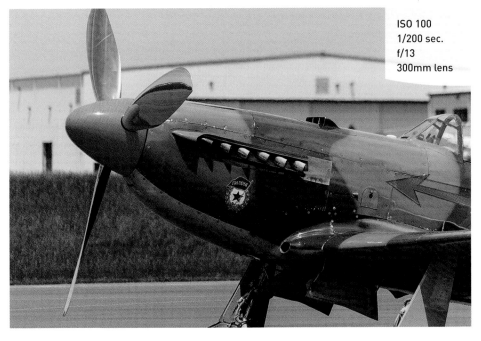

ISO 100
1/200 sec.
f/13
300mm lens

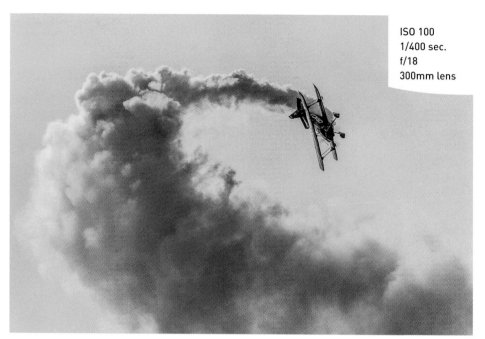

ISO 100
1/400 sec.
f/18
300mm lens

FIGURE 2.8
The long telephoto helped me get a tighter crop on this aerial acrobatics display.

A *zoom* lens is a great compromise to carrying a bunch of single focal-length lenses (also referred to as "prime" lenses). They can cover a wide range of focal lengths because of the configuration of their optics. However, because it takes more optical elements to capture a scene at different focal lengths, the light must pass through more glass on its way to the image sensor. The more glass, the lower the quality of the image sharpness. The other sacrifice that is made is in aperture. Zoom lenses typically have smaller maximum apertures than prime lenses, which means they cannot achieve a narrow depth of field or work in lower light levels without the assistance of image stabilization, a tripod, or higher ISO settings. (We'll discuss all this in more detail in later chapters.)

The T4i can be purchased with the body only, but many folks will purchase it with a kit lens. The most common kit lens is the 18–55mm IS f/3.5–5.6. Another great lens option for the T4i is the 18–200mm EF-S IS lens. It is a great all-around lens that provides a range of focal lengths, from the very wide to the medium telephoto. Combine that with great image stabilization and you have what I like to call the perfect vacation lens. Unfortunately, it is not available as a kit lens at the moment, but you should definitely consider it if you are thinking of adding a new lens to your camera bag.

WHAT IS EXPOSURE?

In order for you to get the most out of this book, I need to briefly discuss the principles of exposure. Without this basic knowledge, it will be difficult for you to move forward in improving your photography. For our purposes, I will just cover some of the basics of exposure. This will give you the essential tools to make educated decisions in determining how best to photograph a subject.

So what is exposure? It is the process whereby the light reflecting off a subject reflects through an opening in the camera lens for a defined period of time onto the camera sensor. The combination of the lens opening, shutter speed, and sensor sensitivity is used to achieve a proper exposure value (EV) for the scene. The EV is the sum of these components necessary to properly expose a scene. The relationship between these factors is sometimes referred to as the "exposure triangle."

At each point of the triangle lies one of the factors of exposure:

- **ISO:** Determines the sensitivity of the camera sensor. ISO stands for the International Organization for Standardization, but the acronym is used as a term to describe the sensitivity of the camera sensor to light. The higher the sensitivity, the less light is required for a good exposure. These values are a carryover from the days of traditional color and black and white films.

- **Aperture:** Also referred to as f-stop, this determines how much light passes through the lens at once.

- **Shutter Speed:** Controls the length of time that light is allowed to hit the sensor.

So here's how it works. The camera sensor has a level of sensitivity that is determined by the ISO setting. To get a proper exposure—not too much, not too little—the lens needs to adjust the aperture diaphragm (the size of the lens opening) to control the volume of light entering the camera. Then the shutter is opened for a relatively short period of time to allow the light to hit the sensor long enough for it to record on the sensor.

ISO numbers for the T4i start at 100 and then double in sensitivity as you double the number. So 200 is twice as sensitive as 100. The camera can be set to use 1/2- or 1/3-stop increments, but for ISO just remember that the base numbers double: 100, 200, 400, 800, and so on. There are also a wide variety of shutter speeds that you can use to achieve a proper exposure. The speeds on the T4i range from as long as 30 seconds to as short as 1/4000 of a second. When using the camera, you will not see the one over the number while looking through the viewfinder, so you will need to remember that anything shorter than a second will be a fraction. However, the shutter speed is displayed as a fraction when looking at the rear LCD display. Typically, you will be working with a shutter speed range from around 1/30 of a second to about 1/2000, but these numbers will change depending on your circumstances and the effect that you are trying to achieve. The lens apertures will vary slightly depending on which lens you are using. This is because different lenses have different maximum apertures. The typical apertures that are at your disposal are f/4, f/5.6, f/8, f/11, f/16, and f/22.

When it comes to exposure, a change to any one of these factors can require changing one or more of the other two. This is referred to as a reciprocal change. If you let more light in the lens by choosing a larger aperture opening, you will need to shorten the amount of time the shutter is open. If the shutter is allowed to stay open for a longer period of time, the aperture needs to be smaller to restrict the amount of light coming in.

HOW IS EXPOSURE CALCULATED?

We now know about the exposure triangle—ISO, shutter speed, and aperture—so it's time to put all three together to see how they relate to one another and how you can change them as needed.

STOP

You will hear the term *stop* thrown around all the time in photography. It relates back to the f-stop, which is a term used to describe the aperture of your lens. When you need to give some additional exposure, you might say that you are going to "add a stop." This doesn't just equate to the aperture; it could also be used to describe the shutter speed or even the ISO. So when your image is too light or dark or you have too much movement in your subject, you will probably be changing things by a "stop" or two.

When you point your camera at a scene, the light reflecting off your subject enters the lens and is allowed to pass through to the sensor for a period of time dictated by the shutter speed. The amount and duration of the light needed for a proper exposure depends on how much light is being reflected and how sensitive the sensor is. To figure this out, your camera utilizes a built-in light meter that looks through the lens and measures the amount of light. That level is then calculated against the sensitivity of the ISO setting, and an exposure value is rendered. Here is the tricky part: there is more than one way to achieve a perfect exposure, because the f-stop and shutter speed can be combined in different ways to allow the same amount of exposure. See, I told you it was tricky.

Here is a list of reciprocal settings that would all produce the same exposure result. Let's use the "sunny 16" rule, which states that, when using f/16 on a sunny day, you can use a shutter speed that is roughly equal to the ISO setting to achieve a proper exposure. For simplification purposes, we will use an ISO of 100.

RECIPROCAL EXPOSURES: ISO 100

F-STOP	2.8	4	5.6	8	11	16	22
SHUTTER SPEED	1/4000	1/2000	1/1000	1/500	1/250	1/125	1/60

If you were to use any one of these combinations, they would each have the same result in terms of the exposure (i.e., how much light hits the camera's sensor). Also take note that every time we cut the f-stop in half, we reciprocated by doubling our shutter speed. For those of you wondering why f/8 is half of f/5.6, it's because those numbers are actually fractions based on the opening of the lens in relation to its focal length. This means that a lot of math goes into figuring out just what the total area of a lens opening is, so you just have to take it on faith that f/8 is half of f/5.6 but twice as much as f/11. A good way to remember which opening is larger is to think of your camera lens as a pipe that controls the flow of water. If you have a pipe that is 1/2" in diameter (f/2) and one that is 1/8" (f/8), which would allow more water to flow through? It would be the 1/2" pipe. The same idea works here with the camera f-stops; f/2 is a larger opening than f/4 or f/8 or f/16.

Now that we know this, we can start using this information to make intelligent choices in terms of shutter speed and f-stop. Let's bring the third element into this by changing our ISO by one stop, from 100 to 200.

RECIPROCAL EXPOSURES: ISO 200

F-STOP	2.8	4	5.6	8	11	16	22
SHUTTER SPEED	–	1/4000	1/2000	1/1000	1/500	1/250	1/125

Notice that, since we doubled the sensitivity of the sensor, we now require half as much exposure as before. We have also reduced our maximum aperture from f/2.8 to f/4 because the camera can't use a shutter speed that is faster than 1/4000 of a second.

So why not just use the exposure setting of f/16 at 1/250 of a second? Why bother with all of these reciprocal values when this one setting will give us a properly exposed image? The answer is that the f-stop and shutter speed also control two other important aspects of our image: motion and depth of field.

MOTION AND DEPTH OF FIELD

There are distinct characteristics that are related to changes in aperture and shutter speed. Shutter speed controls the length of time the light has to strike the sensor; consequently, it also controls the blurriness (or lack of blurriness) of the image. The less time light has to hit the sensor, the less time your subjects have to move around and become blurry. This can let you do things like freezing the motion of a fast-moving subject (**Figure 2.9**) or intentionally blurring subjects to give the feel of energy and motion (**Figure 2.10**).

ISO 100
1/500 sec.
f/4
280mm lens

FIGURE 2.9
A fast shutter speed was used to freeze the action of the kayaker.

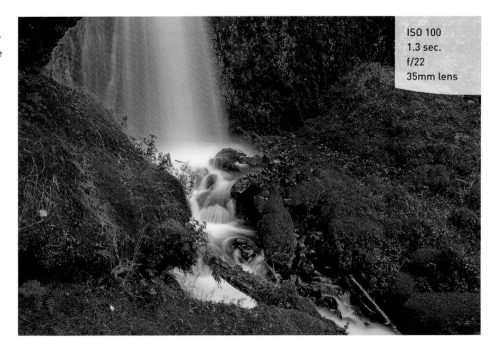

FIGURE 2.10
The slower shutter speed captured the flow of water over the rocks.

ISO 100
1.3 sec.
f/22
35mm lens

The aperture controls the amount of light that comes through the lens, but it also determines what areas of the image will be in focus. This is referred to as depth of field, and it is an extremely valuable creative tool. The smaller the opening (the larger the number, such as f/22), the greater the sharpness of objects from near to far (**Figure 2.11**).

A large opening (or small number, like f/2.8) means more blurring of objects that are not at the same distance from the camera as the subject you are focusing on (**Figure 2.12**).

As we further explore the features of the camera, we will learn not only how to utilize the elements of exposure to capture properly exposed photographs, but also how we can make adjustments to emphasize our subject. It is the manipulation of these elements—motion and focus—that will take your images to the next level.

ISO 400
1/400 sec.
f/16
40mm lens

FIGURE 2.11
By using a small aperture, the area of sharp focus extends from a point that is near the camera all the way out to distant objects. In this instance, I wanted the trees in the foreground as well as the mountains in the background to be in focus.

ISO 200
1/1250 sec.
f/2.8
70mm lens

FIGURE 2.12
Isolating a subject is accomplished by using a large aperture, which produces a narrow area of sharp focus.

VIDEO AND THE T4i

One of the reasons why you might have purchased the T4i is its ability to capture video. Not just regular video, but high-definition video. As I discussed in the book's introduction, I am going to keep the focus of this book on the photography aspects of the camera, but that doesn't mean I am going to simply ignore the video functions. In fact, I am dedicating a bonus chapter to some fun video tips. But I thought that I would at least cover the video basics here in Chapter 2 since we have already looked at a lot of other camera functions. First, let's cover some of the basic facts about the moviemaking features.

The video recording is a separate feature from the Live View capabilities of the camera. To shoot video, you will need to turn the power switch to the Movie Shooting position.

Once Movie mode is active, you will need to focus the camera by placing the white focus box on the subject (**Figure 2.13**) and holding down the shutter button halfway until the focus operation is complete.

Once your subject is in focus, you can push the Live View/Record button to begin the recording process. When the camera begins recording, you will notice that the focus box disappears and a few new icons show up on the LCD. In the upper-right corner will be a red Record icon to let you know that the camera is in active record mode. In the bottom of the screen is an exposure compensation scale and the battery-level indicator. To stop the video recording, simply press the Live View/Record button a second time.

FIGURE 2.13
Recording high-def video with your T4i.

VIDEO QUALITY

The highest-quality video setting on your T4i will render high-definition video with a resolution of 1920 x 1080 or 1280 x 720 pixels. This is also referred to as 1080P and 720P. The "1080" and "720" represent the height of the video image in pixels, and the "P" stands for Progressive, which is how the camera actually records/draws the video on the screen. You can select a lower-resolution video depending on your needs. The other video resolution is 640 x 480. For high-definition TV and computer/media station viewing, you will be served best using the 1080 or 720 recording resolutions. If you plan on recording for the Internet, iPods, standard-definition TV, or portable video players, you might want to consider using the 640 x 480 resolution. The benefit of 640 x 480 is that it requires less physical storage since it contains a smaller pixel count. This means that you will not only fit more video on your storage card, you will also require less time to upload the video to the Internet. Another benefit of the 640 x 480 resolution is that it records for longer than the HD resolutions—almost 30 minutes for 640, as opposed to 10 minutes of recording time for HD.

The other thing to consider when selecting a quality setting is the capture frame rate. At the 1920 x 1080 size, you have two frame rates to choose from: 30 frames per second or 24 frames per second (fps). The 30 fps setting is more of a TV standard and complies with the NTSC video standards used in the United States. This should be your choice for most of your video recording. If you are going to use the video for DVD or for movies with a "Hollywood" look, you should go with the 24 fps option.

The 60 fps on the 1280 x 720 option should render smooth video sequences, but they might also look a little like slow motion. One reason for using this frame rate is that it helps with fast movement of the camera or subject.

PROGRESSIVE SCAN

When it comes to video, there are usually two terms associated with the quality of the video and how it is captured and displayed on a monitor/screen: *progressive* and *interlaced*. The two terms describe how the video is drawn by line for each frame. Video frames are not displayed all at once like a photograph. In progressive video, the lines are drawn in sequence from top to bottom. Interlaced video draws all of the odd-numbered lines and then all of the even-numbered lines. This odd-even drawing can present itself as screen flicker, which is why the progressive video standard is preferred, especially when viewing high-definition images.

SETTING THE MOVIE QUALITY

1. To change the quality of your video recording, start by turning the power switch to the Movie Shooting position.

2. Press the Menu button and navigate to the second movie-shooting tab.

3. Select the Movie record size option, and press the Set button (**A**).

4. Select the desired movie quality setting by pressing the left or right Cross key, and press the Set button (**B**).

5. Press the Menu button to return to Movie mode.

A

B

SOUND

The T4i can record audio to go along with your video, but there are a couple of things to keep in mind when using it. The first is to make sure you don't block the microphone on the front of the camera. If you look closely at the top of the camera body, you will notice some small holes on the top of the camera, just in front of the hot shoe (**Figure 2.14**).

FIGURE 2.14
The T4i's built-in microphone.

The next thing you need to know about the sound is that because the microphone is part of the camera, any noise that the camera makes, such as when it's focusing the lens, will be audible in your movies. If you find that the lens focus noise is distracting or you plan to add your own soundtrack to the video at a later time, you can turn the audio recording off.

TURNING OFF THE SOUND

1. Turn the power switch to the Movie Shooting position.

2. Press the Menu button, navigate to the second movie-shooting tab, highlight Sound recording, and press the Set button (**A**).

3. Select the Disable option, and press Set to lock in the change (**B**). Press the Menu button to return to recording mode.

A

B

BETTER SOUND FOR YOUR MOVIES

If you want to eliminate the camera noise that comes with recording sound with your camera, you should consider using an external microphone. You can have much more control over the quality of the audio because you are using a device whose sole purpose is to record audio. There is a growing market of microphones for DSLR cameras, including mics with hot shoe adapters that allow you to mount the mic to the camera so you can record without having to worry about holding the external mic (**Figure 2.15**).

Another advantage of using external microphones is that you can use ones that are designed to do a better job of recording directional audio, such as that coming from subjects in front of the camera. Most of these microphones are long and slender and are referred to as shotgun mics.

FIGURE 2.15
Using an external microphone like this model from Rode will help eliminate camera noise from your videos.

FOCUSING THE CAMERA

As mentioned, you must focus the camera using the shutter release button before you will be able to start recording video. Once the video is recording, you can refocus using the same button. If your subject moves closer to or farther from the camera position, it will be necessary for you to refocus in order to maintain sharp focus. A great new feature in the T4i is the Movie-Servo autofocus system, which will use autofocus to follow your subject. The default setting for Movie-Servo is ON, so there is no need to activate it in the menu. You can even pause it while shooting by making sure the AE/AF Lock/Focus/Reduce Image button is set to AF/AF Lock, not AE Lock, in the custom menu. After setting the function, you can pause Movie-Servo mode by pressing and holding the AE/AF Lock/Focus/Reduce Image button. The Movie-Servo autofocus will resume once you release the button. You can manually focus your lens by setting the focus switch on the lens to the MF position and then turning the focus ring on the lens. If you have your camera set to Movie-Servo, be sure to turn the camera off prior to setting the lens to the MF mode.

AE/AF LOCK/FOCUS/REDUCE IMAGE BUTTON

The AE/AF Lock/Focus/Reduce Image button can perform a number of functions depending on what it is you are doing. To locate the button, look at item F in the Chapter 1 Camera Back illustration.

For more about focusing while shooting movies, be sure to check out the bonus chapter "T4i Video: Beyond the Basics."

CAPTURING VIDEO SNAPSHOTS

So, what if you don't need more than a short video clip, say, 4 seconds or so? Or perhaps you want a longer sequence that is made up of smaller video clips. Well, you might want to consider setting up the Video Snapshot feature. When this is activated, you can be in Movie mode and then press the Record button to grab a small snippet of video (2, 4, or 8 seconds in length). Once the camera has completed recording, you can save the clip to an album. You can add additional video snapshot clips to the album to create one longer video from the snapshots. This feature allows you to make some very creative video sequences right in your camera.

ACTIVATING VIDEO SNAPSHOTS

1. Set the camera to Movie mode.

2. Press the Menu button and navigate to the second movie-shooting tab.

3. Use the down Cross key to select Video snapshot, and press Set (**A**).

4. Select Video snapshot, press the Set button, and then select Enable (**B**).

5. Next, select Album settings (**C**), press Set, and then select Create a new album.

6. Once you have created a new album, select a clip length of 2, 4, or 8 seconds (**D**).

7. Exit the menu by pressing the Menu button.

8. Set up your movie shooting just like you normally would, and press the Record button to begin the recording process. The video recording will cease once the time limit has been reached.

9. Now you can add the clip to your album, save it as a new album, play back the video, or delete it without saving (**E**).

WATCHING YOUR VIDEOS

There are a couple of different options you can use to review your video once you have finished recording. The first is probably the easiest: press the Image Review button to bring up the recorded image on the LCD screen, and then use the Set button to start playing the video. The left/right Cross keys act as the video controller and allow you to rewind and fast-forward as well as stop the video altogether.

FIGURE 2.16
The video ports on the T4i.

If you would like to get a larger look at things, you will need to either watch the video on your TV or move the video files to your computer. To watch on your TV, you can use the video cable that came with your camera and plug it in to the small port on the side of the camera body (**Figure 2.16**). This will let you watch low-resolution video on your TV. To get the full effect from your HD videos, you will need to purchase an HDMI cable (your TV needs to support at least 720 HD and have an HDMI port to use this option). Make sure that you purchase a Mini-HDMI-to-HDMI cable since the camera does not use a standard-sized HDMI jack for outputting video. Once you have the cable hooked up to your TV, simply use the same camera controls that you used for watching the video on the LCD screen.

If you want to watch or use the videos on your computer, you will need to download the images by using the Canon software or by using an SD card reader attached to your computer. The video files will have the extension ".mov" at the end of the file name. These files should play on either a Mac or a Windows PC using software that came with your operating system or that can be downloaded for free

Manual Callout

You can check out all of the video features of your camera by turning to pages 169–197 of your owner's manual.

(Apple's QuickTime for Mac and Windows is available at www.apple.com/quicktime/download/). If you are using an SDXC card, make sure that you have a compatible card reader to attach to your computer.

For even more information about using video with your T4i, be sure to download the bonus chapters from Peachpit.com.

Chapter 2 Assignments

Formatting your card

Even if you have already begun using your camera, make sure you are familiar with formatting the SD card. If you haven't done so already, follow the directions given earlier in the chapter and format as described (make sure you save any images that you may have already taken). Then perform the Format function every time you have downloaded or saved your images or use a new card.

Checking your firmware version

Using the most up-to-date version of the camera firmware will ensure that your camera is functioning properly. Use the menu to find your current firmware version, and then update as necessary using the steps listed in this chapter.

Cleaning your sensor

You probably noticed the sensor-cleaning message the first time you turned your camera on. Make sure you are familiar with the Clean Now command so you can perform this function every time you change a lens.

Exploring your image formats

I want you to become familiar with all of the camera features before using the RAW format, but take a little time to explore the format menu so you can see what options are available to you.

Exploring your lens

If you are using a zoom lens, spend a little time shooting with all of the different focal lengths, from the widest to the longest. See just how much of an angle you can cover with your widest lens setting. How much magnification will you be able to get from the telephoto setting? Try shooting the same subject with a variety of different focal lengths to note the differences in how the subject looks, and also the relationship between the subject and the other elements in the photo.

Recording some video clips

Take a little time to discover how the video function works on your camera. Set the video quality to 1080 and record a short sequence, and then try it with some of the lower-resolution settings. Open the video clips on your computer or hook the camera up to your TV and review the different video clips to see how the quality settings affect the video.

Share your results with the book's Flickr group!

Join the group here: flickr.com/groups/t4i650dfromsnapshotstogreatshots

3

ISO 400
1/800 sec.
f/5
18mm lens

The Basic Zone

GET SHOOTING WITH THE AUTOMATIC CAMERA MODES

The Canon T4i is an amazing camera that has some incredible features. In fact, with all of the technology built into it, it can be pretty intimidating for the person new to DSLR photography. For that reason, Canon has made it a little easier for you to get some great-looking photographs without having to do a lot of thinking. Enter the Basic zone. The camera modes on the Basic zone side of the Mode dial are simple, icon-labeled modes that are set up to use specific features of the camera for various shooting situations. Let's take a look at the different modes and how and when to use them.

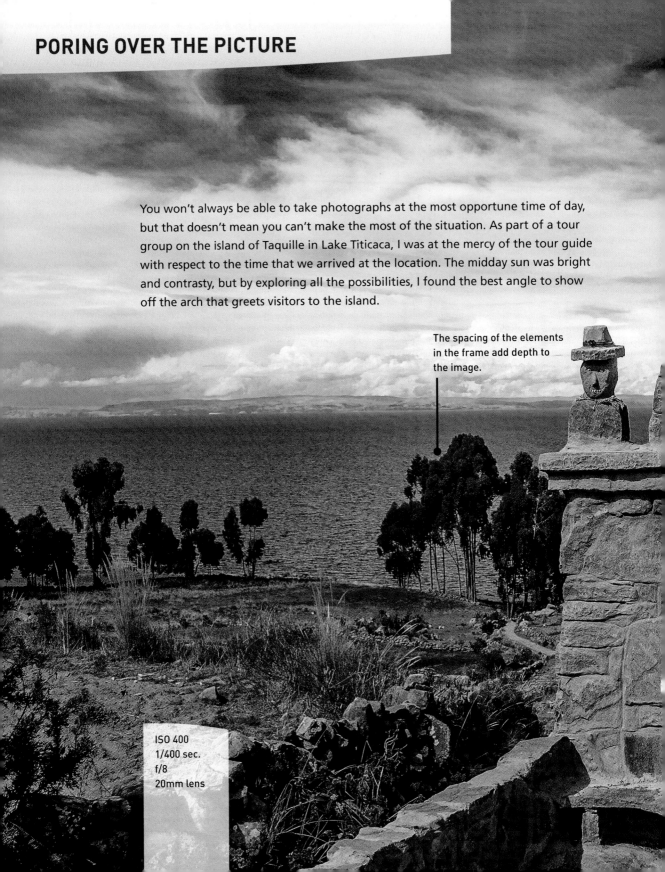

PORING OVER THE PICTURE

You won't always be able to take photographs at the most opportune time of day, but that doesn't mean you can't make the most of the situation. As part of a tour group on the island of Taquille in Lake Titicaca, I was at the mercy of the tour guide with respect to the time that we arrived at the location. The midday sun was bright and contrasty, but by exploring all the possibilities, I found the best angle to show off the arch that greets visitors to the island.

The spacing of the elements in the frame add depth to the image.

ISO 400
1/400 sec.
f/8
20mm lens

I positioned myself so that the sun was at my back to get the most pleasing light on the subject.

An aperture setting of f/8 provided plenty of sharpness for the scene.

The arch was positioned to the right for a more interesting composition.

The Landscape picture style adds saturation to the sky and vegetation.

I included some of the foreground foliage to add depth to the scene.

Sometimes you aren't necessarily looking to make an epic landscape shot—just a memory. That doesn't mean that you can't apply good photographic technique to get a good-looking photo. This image was taken as I was walking around the Golden Gate National Recreation Area with some friends. As I walked down to the water's edge, I grabbed this quick shot of the bridge with the city of San Francisco behind it.

The bright sun meant that a low ISO setting could be used.

The horizon is placed in the lower portion of the frame.

ISO 200
1/60 sec.
f/4.5
50mm lens

SCENE INTELLIGENT AUTO MODE

Scene Intelligent Auto mode is all about thought-free photography. There is little to nothing for you to do in this mode except point and shoot. Your biggest concern when using Scene Intelligent Auto mode is focusing. The camera will utilize the automatic focusing modes to achieve the best-possible focus for your picture. Naturally, the camera is going to assume that the object that is closest to the camera is the one that you want in sharpest focus. Simply press the shutter button down halfway while looking through the viewfinder, and you should see one of the focus points light up over the subject. Of course, putting your subject in the middle of the picture is not always the best way to compose your shot. So wait for the chirp to confirm that the focus has been set, and then, while still holding down the button, recompose your shot. Now just press down the shutter button the rest of the way to take the photo. It's just that easy (**Figures 3.1** and **3.2**). The camera will take care of all your exposure decisions, including when to use flash. You do have one option that can be changed while using this mode, and that is whether or not you want to use the self-timer. To set the camera in self-timer mode, simply press the Q button and then use the Cross keys to select Single shooting, Self-timer with 10-second delay, or the Continuous Self-timer mode (which will take multiple exposures).

FIGURE 3.1
Scene Intelligent Auto mode.

Let's face it: this is the lazy man's mode. But sometimes it's just nice to be lazy and click away without giving thought to anything but preserving a memory. There will be times, though, when you want to use your camera's advanced features, which are tailored to specific shooting environments.

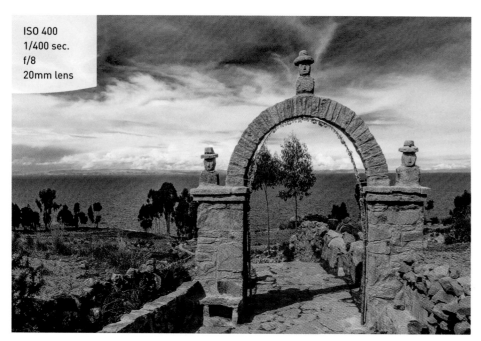

ISO 400
1/400 sec.
f/8
20mm lens

FIGURE 3.2
Scene Intelligent Auto mode works great when you just want to snap some shots without thinking too much, like when I was sightseeing on this Peruvian island.

PORTRAIT MODE

 One problem with Scene Intelligent Auto mode is that it has little idea what type of subject you are photographing and, therefore, is applying the settings based on its "best guess" for each situation. Shooting portraits is a perfect example. When you are taking a photograph of someone, you typically want the emphasis of the picture to be on them, not necessarily on the stuff going on in the background.

This is what Portrait mode is for (**Figure 3.3**). When you set your camera to this mode, you are telling the camera to select a larger aperture so that the depth of field is much

narrower and will give more blur to objects in the background. This blurry background places the attention on your subject (**Figure 3.4**). The other feature of this mode is the automatic selection of the T4i's built-in Portrait picture style (we'll go into more detail about picture styles in later chapters). This style is optimized for skin tones and will also be a little softer to improve the look of skin.

FIGURE 3.3
Portrait mode.

FIGURE 3.4
Portrait mode is
a great choice for
shots like this one.

ISO 200
1/60 sec.
f/5.3
120mm lens

There are some options in this mode that are changeable to your liking. These are
accessed by pressing the Q button on the back of the camera. They include the
Ambience setting, which lets you change the overall look of the image (softer, darker,
warmer, cooler, more vivid, etc.), the white balance, and the shooting drive mode
(Continuous or Self-timer).

USING THE BEST LENS FOR GREAT PORTRAITS

When using Portrait mode, it's usually best to use a lens that is 50mm or longer. The
longer lens will give you a natural view of the subject, as well as aid in keeping the depth
of field narrow.

LANDSCAPE MODE

 As you might have guessed, Landscape mode has been optimized for shooting landscape images. Particular emphasis is placed on the picture style, with the camera trying to boost the greens and blues in the image (**Figures 3.5** and **3.6**). This makes sense, since the typical landscape would be outdoors, where grass, trees, and skies should look more colorful. This picture style also boosts the sharpness that is applied during processing. The camera also utilizes the lowest ISO settings possible in order to keep digital noise to a minimum. The downfall to this setting is that, once again, there is no control over any settings other than the file type and the ability to use the self-timer in 10-second mode.

FIGURE 3.5
Landscape mode.

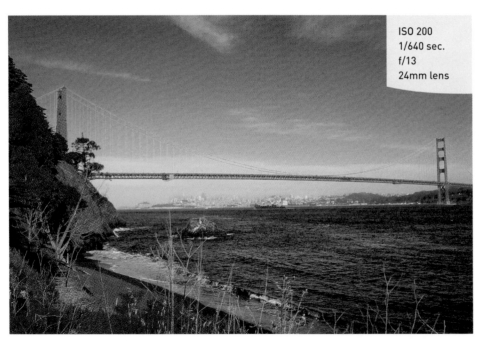

ISO 200
1/640 sec.
f/13
24mm lens

FIGURE 3.6
This type of scene just calls out for Landscape mode. The small aperture helps achieve a greater depth of field.

CLOSE-UP MODE

Although most zoom lenses don't support true "macro" settings, that doesn't mean you can't shoot some great close-up photos. The key here is to use your camera-to-subject distance to fill the frame while still achieving sharp focus. This means moving yourself as close to your subject as you can while still being able to get a good sharp focus. Oftentimes, your lens will be marked with the minimum focusing distance. On my 18–55mm zoom, it is .8 feet. To help get the best focus in the picture, Close-up mode will use the smallest aperture it can while keeping the shutter speed fast enough to get a sharp shot (**Figures 3.7** and **3.8**). It does this by raising the ISO or turning on the built-in flash—or a combination of the two. Unfortunately, we have no way to turn off or alter these adjustments, so it's possible you'll get more digital noise (from a high ISO) or harsh shadows (from the flash) in your picture.

FIGURE 3.7
Close-up mode.

FIGURE 3.8
Close-up mode provided the proper exposure for this old steel door handle.

ISO 200
1/60 sec.
f/11
62mm lens

SPORTS MODE

 Although this is called Sports mode, you can use it for any moving subject that you are photograph-ing. The mode is built on the principles of sports photography: continuous focusing, large apertures, and fast shutter speeds (**Figures 3.9** and **3.10**). To handle these require-ments, the camera sets the drive mode to Continuous shooting, the aperture to a very large opening, and the ISO to Auto. Overall, these are sound settings that will capture most moving subjects well. We will take an in-depth look at all of these features, like Continuous drive mode, in Chapter 5.

FIGURE 3.9
Sports mode.

You can, however, run the risk of too much digital noise in your picture if the camera decides that you need a very high ISO (such as 1600). Also, when using Sports mode, you will need to frame your subject in the middle of the viewfinder so that the cen-ter focus point is on them. You won't hear the familiar chirp or see the focus points illuminate in this mode because, as long as you are holding down the shutter button halfway, the camera will continue to focus on the subject. The only problem with this is that you won't be able to recompose while shooting.

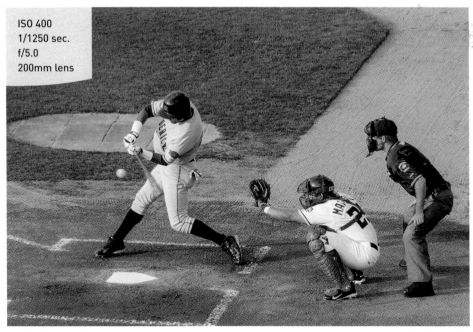

ISO 400
1/1250 sec.
f/5.0
200mm lens

FIGURE 3.10
This is the type of shot that was made for Sports mode, where action-freezing shutter speeds and continuous focusing capture the moment.

NIGHT PORTRAIT MODE

 You're out on the town at night and you want to take a nice picture of someone, but you want to show some of the interesting scenery in the background as well. You could use Scene Intelligent Auto mode, which would probably turn on the flash and take the photo. The problem is that, while it would give you a decent exposure for your subject, the background might end up being completely dark.

FIGURE 3.11
Night Portrait mode.

The solution is to use Night Portrait mode (**Figure 3.11**). When you set the dial to this mode, you are telling the camera that you want to use a slower-than-normal shutter speed so that the background is getting more time (and, thus, more light) to achieve a proper exposure.

The typical shutter speed for using flash is about 1/60 of a second or faster (but not faster than 1/200 of a second). By leaving the shutter open for a longer duration, the camera allows more of the background to be exposed so that you get a much more balanced scene (**Figure 3.12**). This is also a great mode for taking portraits during sunset. Once again, the camera uses an automatic ISO setting, so you will want to keep an eye on it to make sure that setting isn't so high that the noise levels ruin your photo. Also, since your shutter speed will be longer, it's a good idea to use a tripod or place your camera on a stable surface so the background elements don't end up looking shaky.

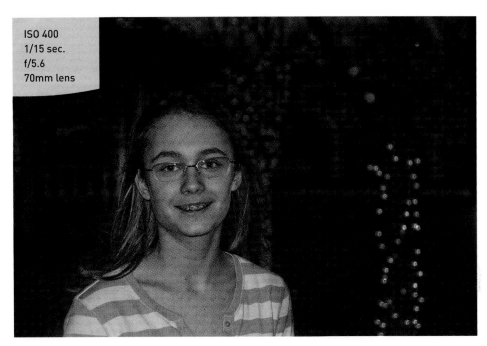

ISO 400
1/15 sec.
f/5.6
70mm lens

FIGURE 3.12
Night Portrait mode uses a slower shutter speed, higher ISO, and larger aperture to balance the background lights with the flash exposure.

FLASH OFF MODE

 Sometimes you will be in a situation where the light levels are low but you don't want to use the flash. It could be that you are shooting in a place that restricts flash photography, such as a museum or church, or it could be that you want to take advantage of the available light, as when shooting candles on a birthday cake. This is where Flash Off mode comes into play (**Figure 3.13**).

	Flash Off
	Flash disabled.
1/60	Note: Dark scenes
F5.0	prone to camera shake.
ISO 100	
	□
Q ⬛	▲L (404)

FIGURE 3.13
Flash Off mode.

By keeping the flash from firing, you will be able to use just the available ambient light while the camera modifies the ISO setting to assist you in getting good exposures (**Figure 3.14**). If the camera feels that the shutter speed is going to be slow enough to introduce camera shake, it will make the shutter speed indicator blink in the view-finder. Fortunately, most of the new image stabilization (IS) lenses being sold today allow you to handhold the camera at much slower shutter speeds and still get great results. The two downfalls to this mode are the Auto ISO setting, which can quickly raise your ISO setting, and the possibility of getting blur from subject movement.

ISO 800
1/13 sec.
f/4.5
70mm lens

FIGURE 3.14
By shooting with the flash off I was able to capture all of the theatrical stage lighting.

CREATIVE AUTO MODE

 Let's face it—these automatic modes in the Basic zone are nice, but there will be times when you want more control over what the camera is doing and how your pictures look. In the Basic zone, this is where the Creative Auto (CA) mode comes in. You won't have total control over the picture-making process, but you will be able to make some adjustments to gain a little more creative control over things like image brightness, use of flash, and background sharpness (**Figure 3.15**).

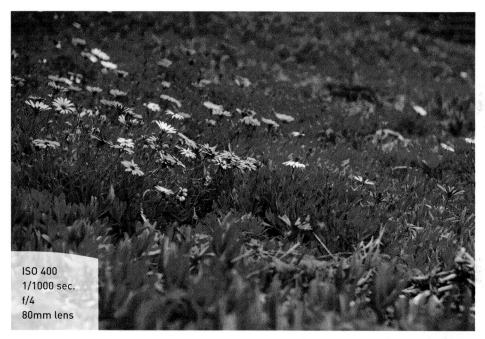

ISO 400
1/1000 sec.
f/4
80mm lens

FIGURE 3.15
Creative Auto mode means you can change how your picture looks, such as creating a shallow depth-of-field effect.

To allow you to make these adjustments, the camera will display on the LCD screen a series of settings that can be changed by pressing the Q button and using the Cross keys and the Main dial (**Figure 3.16**).

FIGURE 3.16
In Creative Auto mode, you see all of the basic shooting information in one easy-to-read screen.

AMBIENCE

If you want to change the look of your picture, you can change the Ambience setting (**Figure 3.17**) and get just the effect you need for your subject. The choices include Standard, Vivid, Soft, Warm, Intense, Cool, Brighter, Darker, and Monochrome. The default setting is Standard, but to change this, press the Q button (or tap the Q icon on the touchscreen), highlight the Ambience selection, change your selection, and press the Set button. You can also control the intensity of the effect that is applied.

FIGURE 3.17
Change the look of your shot with the Ambience feature.

BACKGROUND SHARPNESS

This setting forces the camera to use either a larger or smaller aperture setting to change the depth of field in your image: the smaller the aperture (which means a larger number, such as f/16 or f/22), the greater the sharpness in your background. To change this setting, highlight the Background scale. Then move the index point to the right for a sharper background or to the left for more blur (**Figure 3.18**). Each step will change the exposure by about one f-stop.

FIGURE 3.18
Moving to the right uses a smaller aperture for greater depth of field.

DRIVE MODE

Five drive modes are available in the Creative Auto mode: Single shooting, Continuous shooting, 10-second Self-timer/Remote, 2-second Self-timer, and Continuous Self-timer (**Figure 3.19**). In Single shooting, the camera takes only one picture when the shutter button is depressed all the way. Taking another picture requires releasing the button and then pressing it again. In Continuous shooting, the camera continually takes photographs at about three frames per second until you release the button. You

FIGURE 3.19
You can decide if you want to take one shot at a time or use a more rapid-fire approach.

will probably want to use this setting for capturing action. The third setting available here is the 10-second Self-timer/Remote option. Using this setting allows you to depress the shutter button and have the camera automatically fire 10 seconds later. The obvious use for this setting is to run around and get yourself in the picture. You might also consider using it for macro (close-up) or landscape photography, when you can set your camera on a tripod or a stable surface. The self-timer will let you take the picture without having to worry about camera shake from physically having your hands on the camera while activating the shutter. This is also the mode you should select for using a remote release. Of course, if you are using the self-timer instead of a remote but don't need a long time before the shutter fires, then you should consider the 2-second mode. This option works like the 10-second setting, except you have only a 2-second duration between pressing the shutter and taking the picture. The final mode is Continuous Self-timer, which lets you use the self-timer to take a number of images (from two to ten) with only one press of the shutter release button.

FLASH

This option allows you to set the flash to one of three positions: Auto, On, or Off. In Auto, the flash will automatically pop up whenever the camera determines that there isn't enough light in the scene for a proper exposure. If you want to force the flash to come on no matter what (as when you want to fill in some shadows), set the option to On. The Off setting will keep the flash from firing, just as it does in Flash Off mode (**Figure 3.20**).

FIGURE 3.20
This setting shows the flash in Auto mode.

To make changes to your settings, press the Set button and then use the Cross keys to highlight the item that you want to change. Once highlighted, use the Main dial to select your new setting.

There are two other modes in the Basic zone: Handheld Night Scene and HDR Backlight Control. Since these modes handle specific shooting scenarios, we will cover them later in the book. Look for Handheld Night Scene in Chapter 8 and HDR Backlight Control in Chapter 7.

WHY YOU MAY NEVER WANT TO USE THE BASIC ZONE AGAIN

With so many easy-to-use camera modes, why would anyone ever want to use anything else? Well, the first thing that comes to mind is control. It is the number one reason for using a DSLR camera. The ability to control every aspect of your photography will open up creative avenues that just aren't available in the Basic zone. Let's face it: there is a reason that the Mode dial is split into two different categories. Let's look at what we are giving up when we work in the Basic zone.

- **ISO.** None of the automatic modes in the Basic zone allow you to change the ISO setting from the default of Auto ISO. This will undoubtedly lead to unwanted digital noise in your images when the ISO begins to reach up into the higher settings.

- **Picture style.** If you are using anything but Creative Auto mode, you cannot change the picture style or any of its attributes to fine-tune your images.

- **Color space.** The default is sRGB, and there is no way to change it. If you plan to print any of your pictures, the preferred yet unavailable setting is Adobe RGB.

- **White balance.** There is no choice available for white balance in many of the modes. You are simply stuck with the Auto setting. This isn't always a bad thing, but your camera doesn't always get it right. You can make some adjustments to the lighting or scene type in a few of the basic modes—such as Portrait and Landscape—but not in the fully automatic modes.

- **Auto focus.** Each of the modes uses a specific focus type. Creative Auto, Scene Intelligent Auto, and Flash Off use AI Focus; Sports uses AI Servo; and the remaining modes utilize the One Shot focus mode. There is no way to change these. Even more frustrating is the fact that they all use the Auto Focus Point selection. This means that you can't manually select a focus point, so you must constantly recompose your image.

- **Exposure Compensation.** Only Creative Auto mode allows you to adjust the exposure to brighten or darken your image.

FOCUS MODES ON THE CANON T4I

Three focus modes are available on the T4i. When you're in the Creative zone (discussed in the next chapter), you can easily select the mode that will be most beneficial to the type of photography you're doing. The standard mode is called One Shot, which allows you to focus on one spot and hold the focus until you take the picture or release the shutter button. The AI Servo mode will constantly refocus the camera on your subject the entire time you are depressing the shutter release button; this is great for sports and action photography. The AI Focus mode is a combination of both of the previous modes, using One Shot mode unless the camera senses that the subject is moving, when it will switch to AI Servo mode.

Chapter 3 Assignments

These assignments will have you shooting in the various Basic modes so that you can experience the advantages and disadvantages of using them in your daily photography.

Shooting in Scene Intelligent Auto mode

It's time to give up complete control and just concentrate on what you see in the viewfinder. Set your camera to Scene Intelligent Auto and practice shooting in a variety of conditions, both indoors and outside. Take notice of the camera settings when you are reviewing your pictures. Try picking a focus and then recomposing before taking the picture.

Checking out Portrait mode

Grab your favorite photogenic person and start shooting in Portrait mode. Try switching between Scene Intelligent Auto and Portrait mode while photographing the same person in the same setting. You should see a difference in the sharpness of the background as well as the skin tones. If you are using a zoom lens, set it to about 50mm if available.

Capturing the scenery with Landscape and Close-up modes

Take your camera outside for some landscape and macro work. Find a nice scene, and with your widest available lens, take some pictures using Landscape mode. Then switch back to Scene Intelligent Auto so you can compare the settings used for each image as well as the changes to colors and sharpness. Now, while you are still outside, find something in the foreground—a leaf or a flower—and switch the camera to Close-up mode. See how close you can get, and take note of the f-stop that the mode uses. Then switch to Scene Intelligent Auto and shoot the same subject.

Stopping the action with Sports mode

This assignment will require that you find a subject that is in motion. That could be the traffic in front of your home or your child at play. The only real requirement is that the subject be moving. This will be your opportunity to test out Sports mode. There isn't a lot to worry about here—just point and shoot. Try shooting a few frames one at a time, and then hold down the shutter button and shoot a burst of about five or six frames. It will help if your subject is in good available light to start with so that the camera won't be forced to use high ISOs.

Capturing the mood with Night Portrait mode

This time, wait for it to get dark outside and have a friend sit in a location that has an incandescent lamp in the background (not too bright, though). Switch the camera to Night Portrait, and then, using a wide enough angle to see the subject and some of the room in the background, take a photo. The goal is to get a well-lit picture of your subject and balance that with the light from the lamp in the background. For a comparison, switch the camera back to Scene Intelligent Auto and shoot the same subject. Take notice of the difference in the brightness of the background. Now, take another picture with the camera set to Flash Off, but this time, have your subject sit near the lamp so that it lights up their face. Ask them to sit as still as possible while you hold the camera as still as possible.

Getting a little more creative with Creative Auto mode

Now it's time to have a little fun exploring the options that are available to you using the Creative Auto shooting mode. Get a feel for navigating through the options. Then, working your way down the screen, start making adjustments to each option, taking a picture with each to see how it affects the final photo. The key here is to select one scene and then use it for each change in your settings. This will give you a reference for how each of the images will be affected by changing the options. Try using more than one option to fine-tune your photos.

Share your results with the book's Flickr group!

Join the group here: flickr.com/groups/t4i650dfromsnapshotstogreatshots

4

ISO 200
1/500 sec.
f/11
82mm lens

The Creative Zone

TAKING YOUR PHOTOGRAPHY TO THE NEXT LEVEL

The Creative zone is the name given by Canon to the shooting modes that offer you the greatest amount of control over your photography. To anyone who has been involved with photography for any period of time, these modes are known as the backbones of photography. They allow you to influence two of the most important factors for taking great photographs: *aperture* and *shutter speed*. To access these modes, you simply turn the Mode dial to the Creative mode of your choice and begin shooting. But wouldn't it be nice to know exactly what those modes control and how to make them do our bidding? Well, if you really want to take that next step in controlling your photography, it is essential that you understand not only how to control these modes, but why and when to adjust them so that you get the results you want. So let's move that Mode dial to the first of our Creative modes: Program mode.

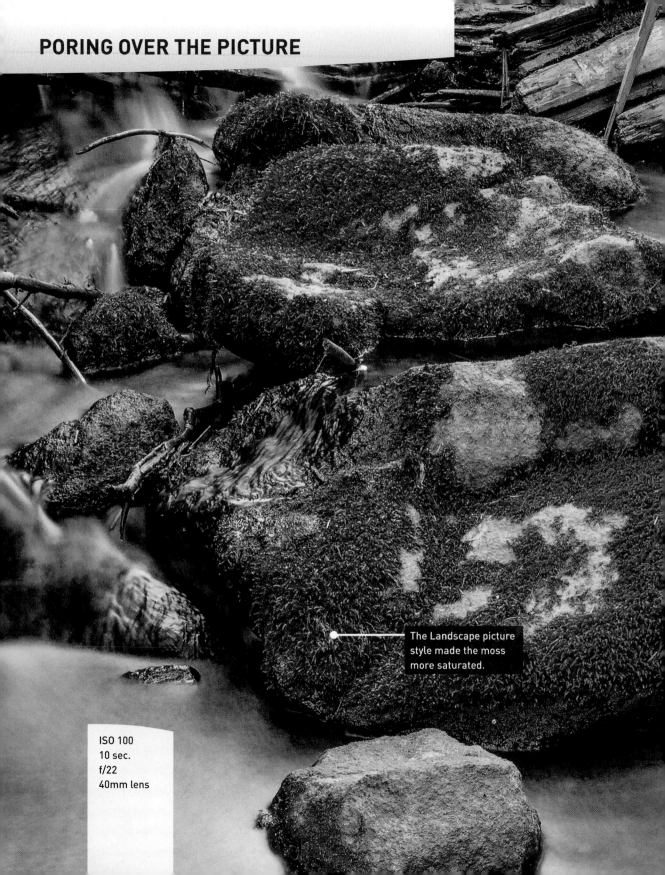

PORING OVER THE PICTURE

The Landscape picture style made the moss more saturated.

ISO 100
10 sec.
f/22
40mm lens

Photographing moving water is not hard, which is probably why I enjoy doing it so much. The real key is finding a location that has good compositional elements. This particular stream had great elements like the small water cascades, the swirling pools, and the mossy rocks, which added great color contrast to the scene.

Using a low ISO setting also helped in getting a long exposure.

A very small aperture was used to get good sharpness.

I used a very long exposure to ensure that the flowing water looked silky smooth.

The flower was arranged to the left of center for a more interesting composition.

I used the selective focus point to get the camera to focus on just the right spot without having to move the camera.

I know it's not very manly, but I have to tell you: I have a thing for flowers. I'm not much into growing them or having them around the house—I prefer to photograph them. With so many varieties and ways of lighting and photographing them, they are always presenting me with new challenges. I spotted this flower in a small garden outside my hotel room in Ollantaytambo, Peru. It had rained the night before, and I loved the small water droplets on the petals and the contrast of the flower against the darker green plant in the background.

I had to set the exposure compensation to –2/3 because of the darker background.

The ISO was raised to help get a small aperture with a shutter speed that was fast enough to handhold the camera.

ISO 400
1/125 sec.
f/9
200mm lens

P: PROGRAM MODE

 There is a reason that Program mode is only one click away from the Basic modes: with respect to apertures and shutter speeds, the camera is doing most of the thinking for you. So, if that is the case, why even bother with Program mode? First, let me say that it is very rare that I will use Program mode, because it just doesn't give as much control over the image-making process as the other Creative modes. There are occasions, however, when it comes in handy, like when I am shooting in widely changing lighting conditions and don't have the time to think through all of my options, or when I'm not very concerned with having ultimate control of the scene. Think of a picnic outdoors in a partial shade/sun environment—I want great-looking pictures, but I'm not looking for anything to hang in a museum. If that's the scenario, why choose Program over one of the Basic modes? Because it gives me choices and control that none of the Basic modes, including Creative Auto, can deliver.

Manual Callout

To see a comparison of all of the different modes in the Basic and Creative zones, check out the tables on pages 310–311 of your owner's manual.

WHEN TO USE PROGRAM (P) MODE INSTEAD OF THE BASIC ZONE MODES

- When shooting in a casual environment where quick adjustments are needed

- When you want control over the ISO

- If you want or need to shoot in the Adobe RGB color space

- If you want to make corrections to the white balance

Let's go back to our picnic scenario. As I said, the light is moving from deep shadow to bright sunlight, which means that the camera is trying to balance our three photo factors (ISO, aperture, and shutter speed) to make a good exposure. From Chapter 1, we know that Auto ISO is just not a consideration, so we have already turned that feature off (you did change it, didn't you?). Well, in Program mode, you can choose which ISO you would like the camera to base its exposure on. The lower the ISO number, the better the quality of our photographs, but the less light sensitive the camera becomes. It's a balancing act, with the main goal always being to keep the ISO as low as possible—too low an ISO, and we will get camera shake in our images from a long shutter speed; too high an ISO means we will have an unacceptable amount of digital noise. For our purposes, let's go ahead and select ISO 400 so that we provide enough sensitivity for those shadows while allowing the camera to use shutter speeds that are fast enough to stop motion.

STARTING POINTS FOR ISO SELECTION

There is a lot of discussion concerning ISO in this and other chapters, but it might be helpful if you know where your starting points should be for your ISO settings. The first thing you should always try to do is use the lowest possible ISO setting. That being said, here are some good starting points for your ISO settings:

- 100: Bright, sunny day
- 200: Hazy, or outdoor shade on a sunny day
- 400: Indoor lighting at night or cloudy conditions outside
- 800: Late night, low-light conditions or sporting arenas at night

These are just suggestions, and your ISO selection will depend on a number of factors that will be discussed later in the book. You might have to push your ISO even higher as needed, but at least now you know where to start.

With the ISO selected, we can now make use of the other controls built into Program mode. By rotating the Main dial, we have the ability to shift the program settings. Remember, your camera is using the internal light meter to pick what it believes are suitable exposure values, but sometimes it doesn't know what it's looking at and how you want those values applied (**Figures 4.1** and **4.2**). With the program shift, you can influence what the shot will look like. Do you need faster shutter speeds in order to stop the action? Just turn the Main dial clockwise. Do you want a smaller aperture so that you get a narrow depth of field? Then turn the dial counterclockwise until you get the desired aperture. The camera shifts the shutter speed and aperture accordingly in order to get a proper exposure, and you will get the benefit of your choice as a result.

FIGURE 4.1
(left) This is my first shot using Program mode. Because I was pointing the camera more toward the ground, the exposure was longer.

FIGURE 4.2
(right) Because I zoomed out and included more of the bright sky in the photo, there was less of the ground to influence the light meter, resulting in a change of exposure.

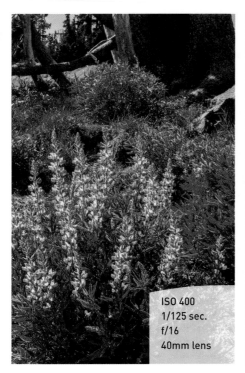

ISO 400
1/125 sec.
f/16
40mm lens

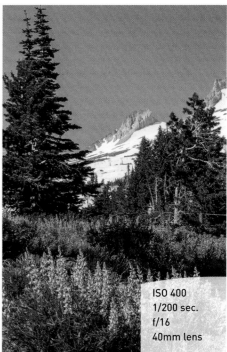

ISO 400
1/200 sec.
f/16
40mm lens

Let's set up the camera for Program mode and see how we can make all of this come together.

SETTING UP AND SHOOTING IN PROGRAM MODE

1. Turn your camera on and then turn the Mode dial to align the P with the indicator line.

2. To select your ISO, press the ISO button on the top of the camera, turn the Main dial to the desired setting, and press the ISO button again (the ISO selection will appear in the rear LCD panel).

3. Point the camera at your subject and then activate the camera meter by depressing the shutter button halfway.

4. View the exposure information in the bottom of the viewfinder or in the display panel on the back of the camera.

5. While the meter is activated, use your index finger to roll the Main dial left and right to see the changed exposure values.

6. Select the exposure that is right for you and start shooting. (Don't worry if you aren't sure what the right exposure is. We will start working on making the right choices for those great shots beginning with the next chapter.)

TV: SHUTTER PRIORITY MODE

Tv mode is what we photographers commonly refer to as Shutter Priority mode. If you dig deep in your manual, you will see that Tv stands for Time Value. I'm not sure who came up with this term, but I can tell you that it wasn't a photographer. In all my years of shooting, I don't ever recall thinking, "Hey, this would be a great situation to use the Time Value mode." But you don't need to know why it is called Tv mode; the important thing is to know why and when to use it.

Like Program mode, Tv mode gives us more freedom to control certain aspects of our photography. In this case, we are talking about shutter speed. The selected shutter speed determines just how long you expose your camera's sensor to light. The longer it remains open, the more time your sensor has to gather light. The shutter speed also, to a large degree, determines how sharp your photographs are. This is different from the image being sharply in focus. Two of the major influences on the sharpness of an image are camera shake and the subject's movement. Because a slower shutter speed means that light from your subject is hitting the sensor for a longer period of time, any movement by you or your subject will show up in your photos as blur.

SHUTTER SPEEDS

A *slow* shutter speed refers to leaving the shutter open for a long period of time—like 1/30 of a second or longer. A *fast* shutter speed means that the shutter is open for a very short period of time—like 1/250 of a second or less.

WHEN TO USE SHUTTER PRIORITY (TV) MODE

- When working with fast-moving subjects where you want to freeze the action (**Figure 4.3**); much more on this in Chapter 5

- When you want to emphasize movement in your subject with motion blur (**Figure 4.4**)

- When you want to use a long exposure to gather light over a long period of time (**Figure 4.5**); more on this in Chapter 8

- When you want to create silky-looking water in a waterfall (**Figure 4.6**)

FIGURE 4.3
Even the fastest of subjects can be frozen with the right shutter speed.

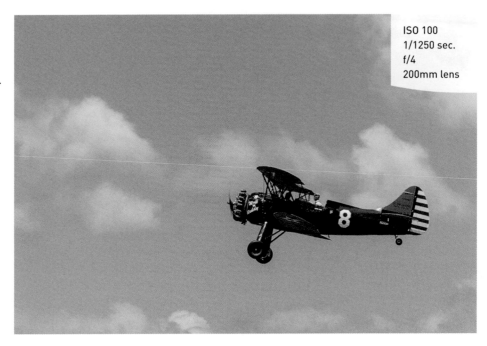

ISO 100
1/1250 sec.
f/4
200mm lens

FIGURE 4.4
Slowing down the shutter speed allows your photographs to convey a sense of movement.

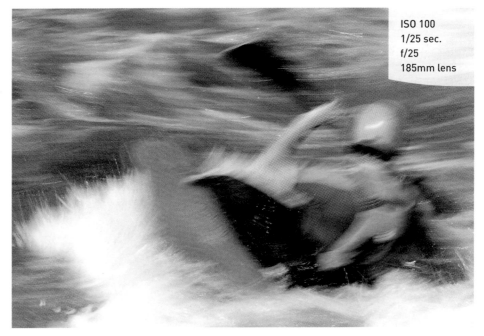

ISO 100
1/25 sec.
f/25
185mm lens

ISO 400
30 sec.
f/22
34mm lens

FIGURE 4.5
A long exposure combined with a small aperture and a steady tripod helped capture this cityscape of San Diego.

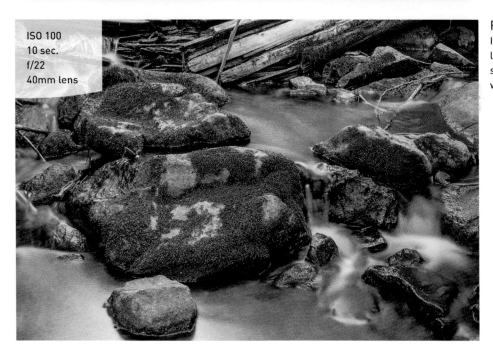

ISO 100
10 sec.
f/22
40mm lens

FIGURE 4.6
Increasing the length of the exposure gives flowing water a silky look.

As you can see, the subject of your photo usually determines whether or not you will use Tv mode. It is important that you be able to visualize the result of using a particular shutter speed. The great thing about shooting with digital cameras is that you get instant feedback by checking your shot on the LCD screen. But what if your subject won't give you a do-over? Such is often the case when shooting sporting events. It's not like you can ask the quarterback to throw that touchdown pass again because your last shot was blurry from a slow shutter speed. This is why it's important to know what those speeds represent in terms of their ability to stop the action and deliver a blur-free shot.

First, let's examine just how much control you have over the shutter speeds. The T4i has a shutter speed range from 1/4000 of a second all the way down to 30 seconds. With that much latitude, you should have enough control to capture almost any subject. The other thing to think about is that Tv mode is considered a "semiautomatic" mode. This means that you are taking control over one aspect of the total exposure while the camera handles the other. In this instance, you are controlling the shutter speed and the camera is controlling the aperture. This is important to know because there will be times that you want to use a particular shutter speed but your lens won't be able to accommodate your request.

For example, you might encounter this problem when shooting in low-light situations: if you are shooting a fast-moving subject that will blur at a shutter speed slower than 1/125 of a second but your lens's largest aperture is f/3.5, you might see your aperture display in the viewfinder and the rear LCD panel begin to blink. This is your warning that there won't be enough light available for the shot—due to the limitations of the lens—so your picture will be underexposed (too dark).

Another case where you might run into this situation is when you are shooting moving water. To get that look of silky, flowing water, it's usually necessary to use a shutter speed of at least 1/15 of a second, if not longer. If your waterfall is in full sunlight, you may get that blinking aperture display once again because the lens you are using only closes down to f/22 at its smallest opening. In this instance, your camera is warning you that you will be overexposing your image (too light). There are workarounds for these problems, which we will discuss later (see Chapter 7), but it is important to know that there can be limitations when using Tv mode.

SETTING UP AND SHOOTING IN TV MODE

1. Turn your camera on and then turn the Mode dial to align the Tv with the indicator line.
2. Select your ISO by pressing the ISO button on the top of the camera and then turning the Main dial (the ISO selection will appear in the rear LCD panel).

3. Point the camera at your subject and then activate the camera meter by depressing the shutter button halfway.

4. View the exposure information in the bottom area of the viewfinder or in the rear LCD panel.

5. While the meter is activated, use your index finger to roll the Main dial left and right to see the changed exposure values. Roll the dial to the right for faster shutter speeds and to the left for slower speeds.

AV: APERTURE PRIORITY MODE

You wouldn't know it from its name, but Av mode is one of the most useful and popular modes in the Creative zone. Av stands for Aperture Value, and like Time Value, it's another term that you'll seldom hear a photographer toss around. The mode, however, is one of my favorites, and I believe that it will quickly become one of yours as well. Av, more commonly referred to as Aperture Priority mode, is also deemed a semiautomatic mode because it allows you to once again control one factor of exposure while the camera adjusts for the other.

Why, you may ask, is this one of my favorite modes? It's because the aperture of your lens dictates depth of field. Depth of field, along with composition, is a major factor in how you direct attention to what is important in your image. It is the factor that controls how much of your image is in focus. If you want to isolate a subject from the background, such as when shooting a portrait, you can use a large aperture to keep the focus on your subject and make both the foreground and background blurry. If you want to keep the entire scene sharply focused, such as with a landscape, then using a small aperture will render the greatest possible depth of field.

WHEN TO USE APERTURE PRIORITY (AV) MODE

- When shooting portraits or wildlife (**Figure 4.7**)

- When shooting most landscape photography (**Figure 4.8**)

- When shooting macro, or close-up, photography (**Figure 4.9**)

- When shooting architectural photography, which often benefits from a large depth of field (**Figure 4.10**)

FIGURE 4.7
A fairly large aperture coupled with a long focal length created a very blurry background, so all the emphasis was left on the subject.

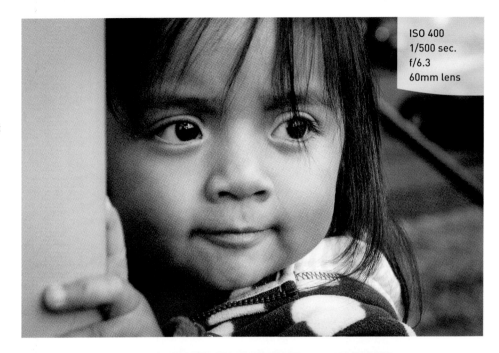

ISO 400
1/500 sec.
f/6.3
60mm lens

FIGURE 4.8
The smaller aperture setting brings sharpness to near and far objects.

ISO 400
1/60 sec.
f/14
35mm lens

ISO 400
1/125 sec.
f/9
200mm lens

FIGURE 4.9
Small apertures give more sharpness in macro images.

ISO 200
1/320 sec.
f/9
27mm lens

FIGURE 4.10
A wide-angle lens combined with a small aperture makes for a large depth of field.

F-STOPS AND APERTURE

As discussed earlier, when referring to the numeric value of your lens aperture, you will find it described as an *f-stop*. The f-stop is one of those old photography terms that, technically, relates to the focal length of the lens (e.g., 200mm) divided by the effective aperture diameter. These measurements are defined as "stops" and work incrementally with your shutter speed to create proper exposure. Older camera lenses used one-stop increments to assist in exposure adjustments, such as 1.4, 2, 2.8, 4, 5.6, 8, 11, 16, and 22. Each stop represents about half the amount of light entering the lens iris as the larger stop before it. Today, most lenses don't have f-stop markings since all adjustments to this setting are performed via the camera's electronics. The stops are also now typically divided into 1/3-stop increments to allow much finer adjustments to exposures, as well as to match the incremental values of your camera's ISO settings, which are also adjusted in 1/3-stop increments.

We have established that Aperture Priority (Av) mode is highly useful in controlling the depth of field in your image. But it's also pivotal in determining the limits of available light that you can shoot in. Different lenses have different maximum apertures. The larger the maximum aperture, the less light you need in order to achieve a properly exposed image. You will recall that, when in Tv mode, there is a limit at which you can handhold your camera without introducing movement or hand shake, which causes blurriness in the final picture. If your lens has a larger aperture, you can let in more light all at once, which means that you can use faster shutter speeds. This is why lenses with large maximum apertures, such as f/1.4, are called "fast" lenses.

On the other hand, bright scenes require the use of a small aperture (such as f/16 or f/22), especially if you want to use a slower shutter speed. That small opening reduces the amount of incoming light, and this reduction of light requires that the shutter stay open longer.

SETTING UP AND SHOOTING IN AV MODE

1. Turn your camera on and then turn the Mode dial to align the Av with the indicator line.

2. Select your ISO by pressing the ISO button on the top of the camera and then turning the Main dial.

3. Point the camera at your subject and then activate the camera meter by depressing the shutter button halfway.

4. View the exposure information in the bottom area of the viewfinder or in the rear display panel.

5. While the meter is activated, use your index finger to roll the Main dial left and right to see the changed exposure values. Roll the dial to the right for a smaller aperture (higher f-stop number) and to the left for a larger aperture (smaller f-stop number).

ZOOM LENSES AND MAXIMUM APERTURES

Some zoom lenses (like the 18–55mm kit lens) have a variable maximum aperture. This means that the largest opening will change depending on the zoom setting. In the example of the 18–55mm zoom, the lens has a maximum aperture of f/3.5 at 18mm and only f/5.6 when the lens is zoomed out to 55mm. Fixed-aperture zoom lenses maintain the same maximum aperture throughout the zoom range. They are typically much more expensive than their variable maximum aperture counterparts.

M: MANUAL MODE

Once upon a time, long before digital cameras and program modes, there was manual mode. In those days it wasn't called "manual mode" because there were no other modes. It was just photography. In fact, many photographers, including me, cut their teeth on completely manual cameras. Let's face it—if you want to learn the effects of aperture and shutter speed on your photography, there is no better way to learn than by setting these adjustments yourself. But today, with the advancement of camera technology, many new photographers never give this mode a second thought. That's truly a shame, as not only is it an excellent way to learn your photography basics, it's also an essential tool to have in your photographic bag of tricks.

When you have your camera set to Manual (M) mode, the camera meter will give you a reading of the scene you are photographing. It's your job, though, to set both the f-stop (aperture) and the shutter speed to achieve a correct exposure. If you need a faster shutter speed, you will have to make the reciprocal change to your f-stop. Using any other mode, such as Tv or Av, would mean that you just have to worry about one of these changes, but Manual mode means you have to do it all yourself. This can be a little challenging at first, but after a while you will have a complete understanding of how each change affects your exposure, which will, in turn, improve the way that you use the other modes.

WHEN TO USE MANUAL (M) MODE

- When you need to maintain exposures between different frames for a panorama (**Figure 4.11**)

- When your environment is fooling your light meter and you need to maintain a certain exposure setting (**Figure 4.12**)

- When shooting silhouetted subjects, which requires overriding the camera's meter readings (**Figure 4.13**)

ISO 200
10 sec.
f/22
24mm lens

FIGURE 4.11
Setting the camera on Manual for panorama shots helps to keep the exposure consistent.

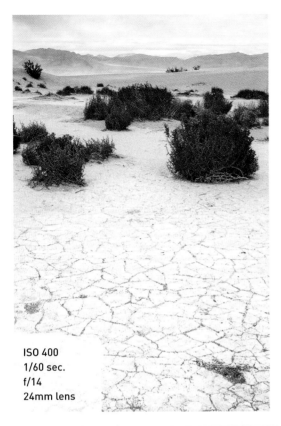

FIGURE 4.12
Bright scenes, such as this dry desert floor in Death Valley, can present a challenge to your light meter.

ISO 400
1/60 sec.
f/14
24mm lens

FIGURE 4.13
I really wanted a silhouette of the cactus needles, so I placed my camera in Manual mode and underexposed the shot.

ISO 100
1/500 sec.
f/9
55mm lens

SETTING UP AND SHOOTING IN MANUAL MODE

1. Turn the Mode dial to align the M with the indicator line.

2. Select your ISO by pressing the ISO button on the top of the camera and then turning the Main dial.

3. Point the camera at your subject and then activate the camera meter by depressing the shutter button halfway.

4. View the exposure information in the bottom area of the viewfinder or in the rear display panel.

5. While the meter is activated, use your index finger to roll the Main dial left and right to change your shutter speed value until the exposure mark is lined up with the zero mark. The exposure information is displayed by a scale with marks that run from –2 to +2 stops. A "proper" exposure will line up with the arrow mark in the middle. As the indicator moves to the left, it is a sign that you will be underexposing (there is not enough light hitting the sensor to provide adequate exposure). Move the indicator to the right and you will be providing more exposure than the camera meter calls for; this is overexposure.

6. To set your exposure using the aperture, depress the shutter release button until the meter is activated. Then, using your thumb, hold in the Av button on the back of the camera, and then use your index finger to turn the Main dial right for a smaller aperture (large f-stop number) or left for a larger aperture (small f-stop number).

HOW I SHOOT: A CLOSER LOOK AT THE CAMERA SETTINGS I USE

The great thing about working with a DSLR camera is that I can always feel confident that some things will remain unchanged from camera to camera. For me, these are the Aperture Priority (Av) and Shutter Priority (Tv) shooting modes. Although I like to think of myself as a generalist in terms of my photography, I do tend to lean heavily on the landscape and urban photography genres. Working in these areas means that I am almost always going to be concerned with my depth of field. Whether it's isolating my subject with a large aperture or trying to maximize the overall sharpness of a sweeping landscape, I always keep an eye on my aperture setting.

If I do have a need to control the action, I use Shutter Priority. If I am trying to create a silky waterfall effect, I can depend on Tv to deliver the long shutter speed that it requires. Maybe I am shooting a motocross jumper—I definitely need the fast shutter speeds that will freeze the fast-moving action. While the other camera modes have their place, I think you will find that, like myself and most other working pros, you will use the Av and Tv modes for 90 percent of your shooting.

The other concern that I have when I am setting up my camera is just how low I can keep my ISO. I raise the ISO only as a last resort because each increase in sensitivity is an opportunity for more digital noise to enter my image. To that end, I always have the High ISO Speed Noise Reduction feature set to Standard (see Chapter 7).

To make quick changes while I shoot, I often use the Exposure Compensation feature (covered in Chapter 7) so that I can make small over- and underexposure changes. This is different than changing the aperture or shutter; it is more like fooling the camera meter into thinking the scene is brighter or darker than it actually is.

One of the reasons I change my exposure is to make corrections when I see the "blinkies" while looking at my images on the rear LCD. Blinkies are the warning signal that part of my image has been overexposed to the point that I no longer have any detail in the highlights. The highlight alert will flash wherever the potential exists for overexposure. The only unfortunate thing about this feature is that it doesn't work with the full-screen preview mode. You have to set your camera display to one of the Histogram modes and then you will see the highlight alert (**Figure 4.14**). If you see any area of the thumbnail blinking black, you are probably overexposing that part of the image.

As you work your way through the coming chapters, you will see other tips and tricks I use in my daily photography, but the most important tip I can give is that you take the time to understand the features of your camera so that you can leverage the technology in a knowledgeable way. This will result in better photographs.

FIGURE 4.14
The T4i's highlight alert screen.

Chapter 4 Assignments

The information covered in this chapter will define how you work with your camera from this point on. Granted, there may be times that you just want to grab some quick pictures and will resort to the Basic zone, but to get serious with your photography, you should learn the modes in the Creative zone.

Starting off with Program mode

Set your camera on Program mode and start shooting. Become familiar with the adjustments you can make to your exposure by turning the Main dial. While shooting, make sure that you keep an eye on your ISO.

Learning to control time with Tv mode

Find some moving subjects and then set your camera to Tv mode. Have someone ride a bike back and forth, or even just photograph cars as they go by. Start with a slow shutter speed of around 1/30 of a second and then start shooting with faster and faster shutter speeds. Keep shooting until you can freeze the action. Now find something that isn't moving, like a flower. Start with your shutter speed at something fast like 1/500 of a second and then work your way down to about 1/4 of a second. The point is to see how well you can handhold your camera before you start introducing hand shake into the image.

Controlling depth of field with Av mode

The name of the game with Av mode is depth of field. Set up three items different distances from you. I would use chess pieces or something similar. Now focus on the middle item and set your camera to the largest aperture that your lens allows (remember that large aperture means a small number, like f/3.5). Now, while still focusing on the middle subject, start shooting with ever-smaller apertures until you are at the smallest f-stop for your lens. If you have a zoom lens, try doing this exercise with the lens at the widest and then the most telephoto settings. Now move up to subjects that are farther away, like telephone poles, and shoot them in the same way. The idea is to get a feel for how each aperture setting affects your depth of field.

Giving and taking with Manual mode

Go outside on a sunny day, and with the camera in Manual mode, set your ISO to 100, your shutter speed to 1/125 of a second, and your aperture to f/16. Now press your shutter release button to get a meter reading. You should be pretty close to that zero mark. If not, make small adjustments to one of your settings until it hits that mark. Now is where the fun begins. Start moving your shutter speed slower, to 1/60, and then set your aperture to f/22. Now go the other way. Set your aperture to f/8 and your shutter speed to 1/500. Now review your images. If all went well, all the exposures should look the same. This is because you balanced the light with reciprocal changes to the aperture and shutter speed. Now go back to our original setting of 1/125 at f/16 and try just moving the shutter speed without changing the aperture. Just make 1/3-stop changes (1/125 to 1/100 to 1/80 to 1/60), and then review your images to see what 1/3 stop of overexposure looks like. Then do the same thing going in the opposite way. It's hard to know if you want to over- or underexpose a scene until you have actually done it and seen the results.

Share your results with the book's Flickr group!

Join the group here: flickr.com/groups/t4i650dfromsnapshotstogreatshots

5

ISO 200
1/1250 sec.
f/5.6
300mm lens

Moving Target

THE TRICKS TO SHOOTING SPORTS AND MORE

Now that you have learned about the Creative zone, it's time to put your newfound knowledge to good use. Whether you are shooting the action at a professional sporting event or a child on a merry-go-round, you'll learn techniques that will help you bring out the best in your photography when your subject is in motion.

The number one thing to know when trying to capture a moving target is that speed is king! I'm not talking about how fast your subject is moving, but rather how fast your shutter is opening and closing. Shutter speed is the key to freezing a moment in time—but also to conveying movement. It's all in how you turn the dial. There are also some other considerations for taking your shot to the next level: composition, lens selection, and a few more items that we will explore in this chapter. So strap on your seatbelt and hit the gas, because here we go!

PORING OVER THE PICTURE

The white balance was set to Auto because of the mixed lighting sources.

Shooting fast-moving subjects is a skill that can take some time to develop. There are so many factors that need to be considered when you set out to photograph a moving object: direction, speed, light, and on and on. The best way to get great shots is to practice, which is why I love shooting the rodeo that comes to the local county fair every year. You won't find a more challenging subject than fast-moving animals under really poor arena lights.

ISO 6400
1/250 sec.
f/2.8
200mm lens

Using AI Servo mode helps keep the subject focused as it moves about.

A high ISO is key to getting a fast shutter speed in low light.

Setting the camera to Continuous shooting mode and taking multiple photos helps increase your chances of getting a great shot.

The bright sunlight meant that I could use a low ISO setting.

Conveying motion can sometimes be a tricky thing in photography. If you use a fast shutter speed, your subject will be frozen but could also look like it was not moving. Learning to change things up a bit can help tell the whole story. This shot is from a series in which I was freezing all the action of the kayakers and the fast-moving water. After shooting a bunch of shots, I got the idea to slow things down and try to include the flow and motion to show how these two forces were battling each other.

WAVE S

To slow down the shutter, I had to use a small aperture setting.

I used a telephoto lens to get in tight on the action.

I had to play with different shutter speeds until I found one that showed motion while still capturing some sharpness in the subject.

ISO 100
1/20 sec.
f/25
185mm lens

STOP RIGHT THERE!

Shutter speed is the main tool in the photographer's arsenal for capturing great action shots. The ability to freeze a moment in time often makes the difference between a good shot and a great one. To take advantage of this concept, you should have a good grasp of the relationship between shutter speed and movement. When you press the shutter release button, your camera goes into action by opening the shutter curtain and then closing it after a predetermined length of time. The longer you leave your shutter open, the more your subject will move across the frame, so common sense dictates that the first thing to consider is just how fast your subject is moving.

Typically, you will be working in fractions of a second. How many fractions depends on several factors. Subject movement, while simple in concept, is actually based on three factors. The first is the direction of travel. Is the subject moving across your field of view (left to right) or traveling toward or away from you? The second consideration is the actual speed at which the subject is moving. There is a big difference between a moving sports car and a child on a bicycle. Finally, the distance from you to the subject has a direct bearing on how fast the action seems to be taking place. Let's take a brief look at each of these factors to see how they might affect your shooting.

DIRECTION OF TRAVEL

Typically, the first thing that people think about when taking an action shot is how fast the subject is moving, but in reality the first consideration should be the direction of travel. Where you are positioned in relation to the subject's direction of travel is critically important in selecting the proper shutter speed. When you open your shutter, the lens gathers light from your subject and records it on the camera sensor. If the subject is moving across your viewfinder, you need a faster shutter speed to keep that lateral movement from being recorded as a streak across your image. Subjects that are moving perpendicular to your shooting location do not move across your viewfinder and appear to be more stationary. This allows you to use a slightly slower shutter speed (**Figure 5.1**). A subject that is moving in a diagonal direction—both across the frame and toward or away from you—requires a shutter speed in between the two.

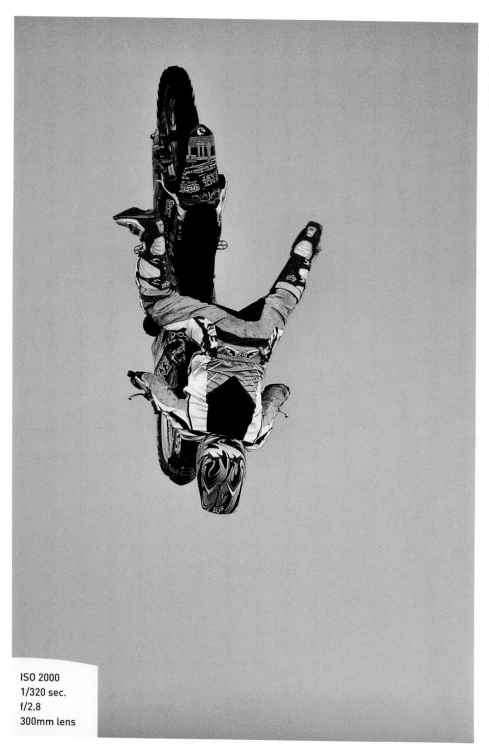

ISO 2000
1/320 sec.
f/2.8
300mm lens

FIGURE 5.1
Action coming
toward the camera
can be captured
with slower
shutter speeds.

SUBJECT SPEED

Once the angle of motion has been determined, you can then assess the speed at which the subject is traveling. The faster your subject moves, the faster your shutter speed needs to be in order to "freeze" that subject (**Figure 5.2**). A person walking across your frame might only require a shutter speed of 1/60 of a second, whereas a cyclist traveling in the same direction would call for 1/500 of a second. That same cyclist traveling at the same rate of speed toward you, rather than across the frame, might only require a shutter speed of 1/125 of a second. You can start to see how the relationship of speed and direction comes into play in your decision-making process.

ISO 1600
1/1000 sec.
f/2.8
300mm lens

FIGURE 5.2
A fast-moving subject that is crossing your path will require a faster shutter speed.

SUBJECT-TO-CAMERA DISTANCE

So now we know both the direction and the speed of your subject. The final factor to address is the distance between you and the action. Picture yourself looking at a highway full of cars from up in a tall building a quarter of a mile from the road. As you stare down at the traffic moving along at 55 miles per hour, the cars and trucks seem to be moving slowly along the roadway. Now picture yourself standing in the median of that same road as the same traffic flies by at the same rate of speed.

Although the traffic is moving at the same speed, the shorter distance between you and the traffic makes the cars look like they are moving much faster. This is because your field of view is much narrower; therefore, the subjects are not going to present themselves within the frame for the same length of time. The concept of distance applies to the length of your lens as well (**Figure 5.3**). If you are using a wide-angle lens, you can probably get away with a slower shutter speed than if you were using a telephoto, which puts you in the heart of the action. It all has to do with your field of view. That telephoto gets you "closer" to the action—and the closer you are, the faster your subject will be moving across your viewfinder.

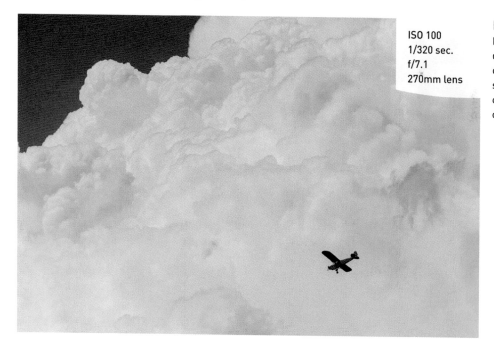

ISO 100
1/320 sec.
f/7.1
270mm lens

FIGURE 5.3
Due to the action's distance from the camera, a slower shutter speed could be used to capture it.

ZOOM IN TO BE SURE

When reviewing your shots on the LCD, don't be fooled by the display. The smaller your image is, the sharper it will look. To ensure that you are getting sharp, blur-free images, make sure that you zoom in on your LCD display.

To zoom in on your images, press the Image Review button located to the lower-right of the LCD display and then press the Magnify Image button to zoom in (**Figure 5.4**). Continue pressing the Magnify Image button to increase the zoom ratio.

To zoom back out, simply press the Reduce Image button (the magnifying glass with the minus sign on it) or press the Image Review button again.

Reduce Image

Magnify Image

Image Review

FIGURE 5.4
Zooming in on your image helps you confirm that the image is really sharp.

USING SHUTTER PRIORITY (TV) MODE TO STOP MOTION

In Chapter 4, you were introduced to the Creative zone's shooting modes. You'll remember that the mode that gives you ultimate control over shutter speed is Tv mode, where you are responsible for selecting the shutter speed while handing over the aperture selection to the camera. The ability to concentrate on just one exposure factor helps you quickly make changes on the fly while staying glued to your viewfinder and your subject.

There are a couple of things to consider when using Tv mode, both of which have to do with the amount of light that is available when shooting. Although you have control over which shutter speed you select in Tv mode, the range of shutter speeds that is available to you depends largely on how well your subject is lit.

When shooting fast-paced action, you will typically be working with very fast shutter speeds. This means that your lens will probably be set to its largest aperture. If the light is not sufficient for the shutter speed selected, you will need to do one of two things: select a lens that offers a larger working aperture, or raise the ISO of the camera. Working off the assumption that you have only one lens available, let's concentrate on balancing your exposure using the ISO.

Let's say that you are shooting a baseball game at night and want to get some great action shots. You set your camera to Tv mode and, after testing out some shutter speeds, determine that you need to shoot at 1/500 of a second to freeze the action on the field. When you place the viewfinder to your eye and press the shutter button halfway, you notice that the f-stop readout is blinking at f/4.5. This is your camera's way of telling you that the lens has now reached its maximum aperture and that you will be underexposed if you shoot your pictures at the currently selected shutter speed. You could slow your shutter speed down until the aperture reading stops blinking, but then you would get images with too much motion blur.

The alternative is to raise your ISO to a level that is high enough for a proper exposure. The key here is to always use the lowest ISO that you can get away with. That might mean ISO 200 in bright, sunny conditions, or ISO 1600 (or higher) for an indoor or night situation (**Figure 5.5**). Just remember that the higher the ISO, the greater the amount of noise in your image. This is the reason that you see professional sports photographers using those mammoth lenses perched atop a monopod: they could use a smaller lens, but to get those very large apertures they need a huge piece of glass on the front of the lens. The larger the glass on the front of the lens, the more light it gathers, and the larger the aperture for shooting. For the working pro, the large aperture translates into low ISO (and thus low noise), fast shutter speeds, and razor-sharp action.

FIGURE 5.5
The only way to stop action under the arena lights and still get a decent shutter speed is to crank up the ISO.

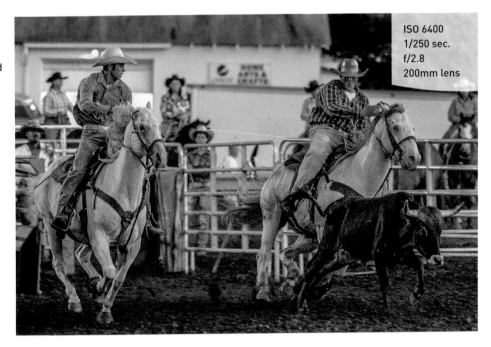

ISO 6400
1/250 sec.
f/2.8
200mm lens

ADJUSTING YOUR ISO ON THE FLY

1. Check for the blinking aperture readout in the lower-right portion of your viewfinder.

2. If it is blinking, move your index finger back from the shutter button and press the ISO button.

3. Now move your finger forward to the Main dial and raise the ISO to the next highest level by turning it to the right.

4. Lightly press the shutter button and check to see if the aperture is still blinking.

5. If it's not blinking, shoot away. If it is, repeat steps 2–4 until it is set correctly.

USING APERTURE PRIORITY (AV) MODE TO ISOLATE YOUR SUBJECT

One of the benefits of working in Tv mode with fast shutter speeds is that, more often than not, you will be shooting with the largest aperture available on your lens. Shooting with a large aperture allows you to use faster shutter speeds, but it also narrows your depth of field.

To isolate your subject in order to focus your viewer's attention on it, a larger aperture is required. The larger aperture reduces the foreground and background sharpness: the larger the aperture, the more blurred they will be.

The reason that I bring this up here is that when you are shooting most sporting events, the idea is to isolate your main subject by having it in focus while the rest of the image has some amount of blur. This sharp focus draws your viewer right to the subject. Studies have shown that the eye is drawn to sharp areas before moving on to the blurry areas. Also, depending on what your subject matter is, there can be a tendency to get distracted by a busy background if everything in the photo is equally sharp. Without a narrow depth of field, it might be difficult for the viewer to estab-lish exactly what the main subject is in your picture.

Let's look at how to use depth of field to bring focus to your subject. In the previous section, I told you that you should use Tv mode for getting those really fast shutter speeds to stop action. Generally speaking, Tv mode will be the mode you most often use for shooting sports and other action, but there will be times when you want to ensure that you are getting the narrowest depth of field possible in your image. The way to do this is by using Aperture Priority (Av) mode.

So how do you know when you should use Av mode as opposed to Tv mode? It's not a simple answer, but your LCD screen can help you make this determination. The best scenario for using Av mode is a brightly lit scene where maximum apertures will still give you plenty of shutter speed to stop the action.

Let's say that you are shooting a soccer game in the midday sun. If you have deter-mined that you need something between 1/500 and 1/1250 of a second for stopping the action, you could just set your camera to a high shutter speed in Tv mode and start shooting. But you also want to be using an aperture of, say, f/4.5 to get that narrow depth of field. Here's the problem: if you set your camera to Tv and select 1/1000 of a second as a nice compromise, you might get that desired f/stop—but you might not. As the meter is trained on your moving subject, the light levels could rise or fall, which might actually change that desired f-stop to something higher like f/5.6

or even f/8. Now the depth of field is extended, and you will no longer get that nice isolation and separation that you wanted.

To rectify this, switch the camera to Av mode and select f/4.5 as your aperture. Now, as you begin shooting, the camera holds that aperture and makes exposure adjustments with the shutter speed (**Figure 5.6**). As I said before, this works well when you have lots of light—enough light so that you can have a high-enough shutter speed without introducing motion blur.

FIGURE 5.6
Because of the large aperture setting, the subjects are nicely separated from the background clutter.

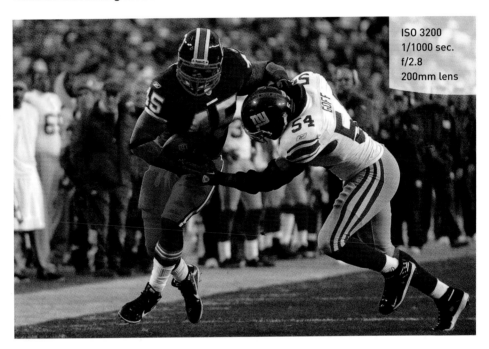

ISO 3200
1/1000 sec.
f/2.8
200mm lens

KEEP THEM IN FOCUS WITH AI SERVO AND AUTO AF POINT SELECTION

With the exposure issue handled for the moment, let's move on to a subject of equal importance: focusing. If you have browsed your manual, you know that there are several focus modes to choose from in the T4i. To get the greatest benefit from each of them, it is important to understand how they work and the situations where each mode will give you the best opportunity to grab a great shot. Because we are discussing subject movement, our first choice is going to be AI Servo mode (the AI stands for Artificial Intelligence). AI Servo uses all of the focus points in the camera to find a moving subject and then lock in the focus when the shutter button is completely depressed. Unlike One Shot, which works best for stationary subjects (such as in portraits or macro work), AI Servo mode will help track your subject in the frame and give you better focus results.

SELECTING AND SHOOTING IN AI SERVO FOCUS MODE

1. Press the right Cross key ("AF" for Automatic Focus) on the back of the camera.

2. Use your index finger to rotate the Main dial until AI Servo appears on the rear LCD panel. You can also use the left and right Cross keys to make the selection. Press the Set button to lock in your change.

3. Locate your subject in the viewfinder, then press and hold the shutter button halfway to activate the focus mechanism.

4. The camera will maintain focus on your subject as long as it remains within one of the focus points in the viewfinder or until you take a picture.

You should also note that the AF mode is used to select the method with which the camera will focus the lens. This is different from the AF point mode, which is a cluster of small points that are visible in the viewfinder and are used to determine where you want the lens to focus (**Figure 5.7**).

When using AI Servo mode, you have the choice of using the Automatic Focus (AF) point mode in automatic, which uses the center point in the viewfinder, or you can select one of the autofocus points as your starting point.

FIGURE 5.7
The Automatic Focus (AF) points are the nine small rectangular boxes arranged in a diamond pattern in your viewfinder.

SELECTING A FOCUS POINT OR USING THE AUTOMATIC FOCUS POINT MODE

1. Press the Focus Point Selection button on the back of the camera. It is the same button you use to zoom in on your image in Preview mode.

2. Rotate the Main dial to move the focus point (you can also use the Cross keys on the back of the camera to quickly jump from one point to the next).

3. You can tell which point is selected by looking at either the rear LCD panel or the illuminated focus points in the viewfinder.

4. To select the Automatic Focus (AF) point mode, rotate the dial until all of the points are either displayed (on the rear LCD panel) or illuminated (in the view-finder). If you are looking at the rear LCD, you will see the words "Automatic selection" above the focus points when the camera is set to auto mode. If a single point has been selected, you will see the words "Manual selection."

5. When you have an individual point selected, the camera will use that specific location to focus the lens. If all the points are selected, the camera will determine what the best source is for focus. The point or points must be on your subject for the autofocus to function properly.

STOP AND GO WITH AI FOCUS

If you are going to be changing between a moving target and one that is still, you should consider using the AI Focus mode. This mode mixes both the One Shot and AI Servo modes for shooting a subject that goes from stationary to moving without having to adjust your focus mode.

When you have a stationary subject, simply place your selected focus point on your subject and the camera will focus on it. If your subject begins to move out of focus, the camera will switch to AI Servo mode and track the movement, keeping a sharp focus.

For example, suppose you are shooting a football game. The quarterback has brought the team to the line and is standing behind the center, waiting for the ball to be hiked. If you are using the AI Focus mode, you can place your focus point on the quarterback and start taking pictures of him as he stands at the line. As soon as the ball is hiked and the action starts, the camera will switch to AI Servo mode and track his movement within the frame. This can be a little tricky at first, but once you master it, it will make your action shooting effortless. Using this mode, you can identify your subject for the camera so that it knows exactly which subject to maintain as the priority for your focus selection.

To select AI Focus, simply follow the same steps listed for selecting AI Servo but instead select the AI Focus mode (**Figure 5.8**).

FIGURE 5.8
Setting your focus mode to AI Focus.

CHOOSING A FOCUS MODE

Selecting the proper focus mode depends largely on what type of subject you are photographing. One Shot is typically best for stationary subjects. It allows you to determine exactly where you want your focus to be and then recompose your image while holding the focus in place. If you are taking pictures of an active subject that is moving quickly, trying to set a focus point with One Shot can be difficult, if not impossible. This is when you will want to rely on the AI modes to quickly assess the subject distance and set your lens focus.

MANUAL FOCUS FOR ANTICIPATED ACTION

While I utilize the automatic focus modes for the majority of my shooting, there are times when I like to fall back on manual focus. This is usually when I know when and where the action will occur and I want to capture the subject as it crosses a certain plane of focus. This is useful in sports like motocross or auto racing, where the subjects are on a defined track. By pre-focusing the camera, all I have to do is wait for the subject to approach my point of focus and then start firing the camera.

In **Figure 5.9**, the horses in the steeplechase race were traveling directly toward me from behind the hedge jump, so tracking it with AI Servo would have been difficult, if not impossible. To get my shot, I simply focused on the front of the hedge and waited for the horses to come into range. As they began their jump over the hedge, I started shooting and captured the horses and riders at the height of the action.

ISO 200
1/4000 sec.
f/2.8
200mm lens

FIGURE 5.9
Pre-focus the camera to a point where you know the subject will be, and start shooting right before they get there.

DRIVE MODES

The drive mode determines how fast your camera will take pictures. Single shooting mode is for taking one photograph at a time. With every full press of the shutter, the camera will take a single image. Continuous mode allows for a more rapid capture rate. Think of it like a machine gun. When you are using Continuous mode, the camera continues to take pictures as long as the shutter release button is held down (or until the memory buffer fills up).

KEEPING UP WITH CONTINUOUS SHOOTING MODE

Getting great focus is one thing, but capturing the best moment on the sensor can be difficult if you are shooting just one frame at a time. In the world of sports, and in life in general, things move pretty fast. If you blink, you might miss it. The same can be said for shooting in Single shooting drive mode. Fortunately, your T4i comes equipped with a Continuous shooting—or "burst"—mode that lets you capture a series of images at up to five frames a second (**Figure 5.10**).

Manual Callout

The number of actual frames that you can capture varies depending on the image format that you are using (JPEG, RAW, or RAW+JPEG). To find out the frame rates, as well as the maximum number of frames that you can take in one continuous burst, check out page 87 of your camera manual.

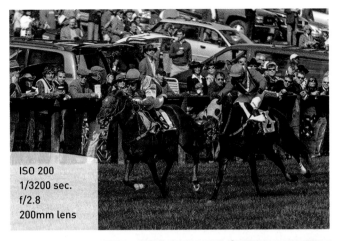

ISO 200
1/3200 sec.
f/2.8
200mm lens

FIGURE 5.10
Using the Continuous drive mode means that you are sure to capture the peak of the action.

SETTING UP AND SHOOTING IN THE CONTINUOUS DRIVE MODE

1. Press the left Cross key on the back of the camera.

2. Rotate the Main dial while looking at the rear LCD screen to select the desired mode. The icon that looks like stacked-up little rectangles is Continuous mode. Press the Set button to lock in your change.

3. To shoot, just depress the shutter button and hold until the desired number of frames has been captured.

Your camera has an internal memory, called a "buffer," where images are stored while they are being processed prior to being moved to your memory card. If the buffer fills up (this is more likely when you are shooting in the RAW or RAW+JPEG format), the camera will stop shooting until space is made in the buffer for new images. If this happens, you will see the word "Busy" in the viewfinder and on the rear LCD panel. The camera readout in the viewfinder tells you how many frames you have available.

A SENSE OF MOTION

Shooting action isn't always about freezing the action. There are times when you want to convey a sense of motion so the viewer can get a feel for the movement and flow of an event. Two techniques you can use to achieve this effect are panning and motion blur.

PANNING

Panning has been used for decades to capture the speed of an object as it moves across the frame. It doesn't work well for subjects that are moving toward or away from you. Panning is achieved by following your subject across your frame, moving your camera along with the subject, and using a slower-than-normal shutter speed so that the background (and sometimes even a bit of the subject) has a sideways blur but the main portion of your subject is sharp and blur-free. The key to a great panning shot is selecting the right shutter speed: too fast and you won't get the desired blurring of the background; too slow and the subject will have too much blur and will not be recognizable. Practice the technique until you can achieve a smooth motion with your camera that follows along with your subject. The other thing to remember when panning is to follow through even after the shutter has closed. This will keep the motion smooth and give you better images.

In **Figure 5.11**, I used the panning technique to follow this cyclist as he rode in front of me. I set the camera drive mode to Continuous shooting, and I used Tv mode to select a shutter speed of 1/40 of a second while the focus mode was on AI Servo.

ISO 100
1/30 sec.
f/22
70mm lens

FIGURE 5.11
Following the subject as it moves across the field of view allows for a slower shutter speed and adds a sense of motion to the shot.

MOTION BLUR

Another way to let the viewer in on the feel of the action is to simply include some blur in the image. This isn't accidental blur from choosing the wrong shutter speed. This blur is more exaggerated, and it tells a story. In **Figure 5.12**, I was interested in capturing the movement of the kayaker as she paddled through the fast-moving water. A fast shutter speed would have surely frozen the action, but it would not have told the story of the movement. Instead of moving with the action, I let the movement of the kayaker and the water create the blur as I held the camera in a stationary position.

FIGURE 5.12
The movement
of the water and
the kayaker, along
with a slow shutter
speed, helps to
convey the action.

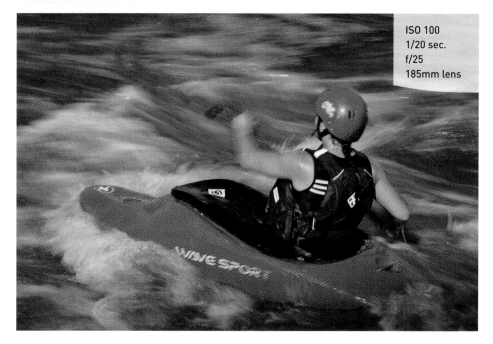

ISO 100
1/20 sec.
f/25
185mm lens

Just as in panning, there is no preordained shutter speed to use for this effect. It is simply a matter of trial and error until you have a look that conveys the action. I usually try to freeze some area of the subject. The key to this technique is the correct shutter speed combined with keeping the camera still during the exposure. You are trying to capture the motion of the subject, not the photographer or the camera, so use a good shooting stance or even a tripod.

TIPS FOR SHOOTING ACTION

GIVE THEM SOMEWHERE TO GO

Whether you are shooting something as simple as your child's soccer match or as complex as the wild motion of a bucking bronco, where you place the subject in the frame is equally as important as how well you expose the image. A poorly composed shot can completely ruin a great moment by not holding the viewer's attention.

The one mistake I see many times in action photography is that the photographer doesn't use the frame properly. If you are dealing with a subject that is moving horizontally across your field of view, give the subject somewhere to go by placing them to the side of the frame, with their motion leading toward the middle of the frame (**Figure 5.13**). This offsetting of the subject will introduce a sense of direction and anticipation for the viewer. Unless you are going to completely fill the image with the action, try to avoid placing your subject in the middle of the frame.

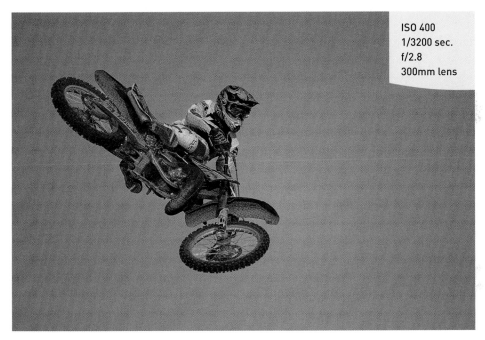

ISO 400
1/3200 sec.
f/2.8
300mm lens

FIGURE 5.13
Try to leave space in front of your subject to lead the action in a direction.

GET IN FRONT OF THE ACTION

Here's another one. When shooting action, show the action coming toward you (**Figure 5.14**). Don't shoot the action going away from you. People want to see faces.

Faces convey the action, the drive, the sense of urgency, and the emotion of the moment. So if you are shooting action involving people, always position yourself so that the action is coming at you or is at least perpendicular to your position.

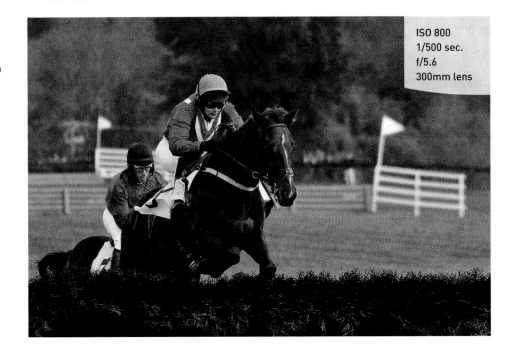

FIGURE 5.14
Shooting from the front with a telephoto gives a feeling that the action is coming right at you.

ISO 800
1/500 sec.
f/5.6
300mm lens

Chapter 5 Assignments

The mechanics of motion

For this first assignment, you need to find some action. Explore the relationship between the speed of an object and its direction of travel. Use the same shutter speed to record your subject moving toward you and across your view. Try using the same shutter speed for both to compare the difference made by the direction of travel.

Wide vs. telephoto

Just as with the first assignment, photograph a subject moving in different directions, but this time, use a wide-angle lens and then a telephoto. Check out how the telephoto setting on the zoom lens will require faster shutter speeds than the lens at its wide-angle setting.

Getting a feel for focusing modes

We discussed two different ways to autofocus for action: AI Servo and AI Focus. Starting with AI Servo mode, find a moving subject and get familiar with the way the mode works. Change from autofocus point selection to a single-point selection.

Now repeat the process using AI Focus mode. The point of the exercise is to become familiar enough with the two modes to decide which one to use for the situation you are photographing.

Anticipating the spot using manual focus

For this assignment, you will need to find a subject that you know will cross a specific line that you can pre-focus on. A street with moderate traffic works well for this. Focus on a spot on the street that the cars will travel across (don't forget to set your lens for manual focus). To do this right, you need to set the drive mode on the camera to Continuous mode. Now, when a car approaches the spot, start shooting. Try shooting in three- or four-frame bursts.

Following the action

Panning is a great way to show motion. To begin, find a subject that will move across your path at a steady speed, and practice following it in your viewfinder from side to side. Now, with the camera in Tv mode, set the shutter speed to 1/30 of a second and the focus mode to AI Servo. Now pan along with the subject and shoot as it moves across your view. Experiment with different shutter speeds and focal lengths. Panning is one of those skills that take some time to get a feel for, so try it with different types of subjects moving at different speeds.

Feeling the movement

Instead of panning with the motion, use a stationary camera position and adjust the shutter speed until you get a blurred effect that gives the sense of motion but still allows the subject to be identified. There is a big difference between a slightly blurred photo that looks like you picked the wrong shutter speed and one that looks intentional for the purpose of showing motion. As with panning, it will take some experimentation to find just the right shutter speed to achieve the desired effect.

Share your results with the book's Flickr group!

Join the group here: flickr.com/groups/t4i650dfromsnapshotstogreatshots

6

ISO 400
1/250 sec.
f/2.8
52mm lens

Say Cheese!

SETTINGS AND FEATURES TO MAKE GREAT PORTRAITS

Taking pictures of people is one of the great joys of photography. You will experience a great sense of accomplishment when you capture the spirit and personality of someone in a photograph. At the same time, you have a great responsibility because the person in front of the camera is depending on you to make them look good. You can't always change how someone looks, but you can control the way you photograph that individual. In this chapter, we will explore some camera features and techniques that can help you create great portraits.

PORING OVER THE PICTURE

Sometimes you find the best photos when you aren't expecting it. As I sat in a waterside restaurant with my family, I saw this young boy throwing his casting net into the water in hopes of catching something to add to his family's dinner pot. The light was coming from behind him, and every time he threw the net it would shimmer in the strong backlight, which added the perfect element to this environmental shot.

The ISO was raised in order to get a fast shutter speed that would freeze the action.

ISO 400
1/800 sec.
f/5.6
220mm lens

A large aperture ensured that the background would be soft, keeping the emphasis on the boy.

The strong backlight required some exposure compensation to lighten the boy.

Using a long lens allowed me to capture the scene from a distance without intruding.

When shooting portraits in outdoor locations, I always look for a variety of backdrop possibilities so that I have options for different lighting conditions. This photo shoot took place in a small park in my city, where I had lots of soft, natural light that was perfect for portraits of this girl.

The subject was framed off-center to improve the composition.

Using a telephoto lens let me crop tightly without having to get in the model's face.

A large aperture helped blur the background.

ISO 400
1/100 sec.
f/5.6
120mm lens

The shady location helped soften the light and reduced harsh shadows.

AUTOMATIC PORTRAIT MODE

In Chapter 3, we reviewed all of the automatic modes in the Basic zone. One of them, Portrait mode, is dedicated to shooting portraits. While this is not my preferred camera setting, it is a great jumping-off point for those who are just starting out. The key to using this mode is to understand what is going on with the camera so that when you venture further into portrait photography, you can expand on the settings and get the most from your camera and, more importantly, your subject.

Whether you are photographing an individual or a group, the emphasis should always be on the subject. Portrait mode utilizes a larger aperture setting to keep the depth of field very narrow, which means that the background will appear slightly blurred or out of focus. To take full advantage of this effect, use a medium- to telephoto-length lens (**Figure 6.1**). Also, keep a pretty close distance to your subject. If you shoot from too far away, the narrow depth of field will not be as effective.

FIGURE 6.1
Portrait mode works best when combined with a medium or long lens.

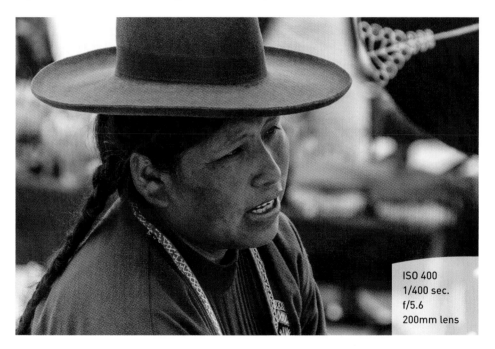

ISO 400
1/400 sec.
f/5.6
200mm lens

USING APERTURE PRIORITY MODE

If you took a poll of portrait photographers to see which shooting mode was most often used for portraits, the answer would certainly be Aperture Priority (Av) mode. Selecting the right aperture is important for placing the most critically sharp area of the photo on your subject, while simultaneously blurring all of the distracting background clutter (**Figure 6.2**). Not only will a large aperture give the narrowest depth of field, it will also allow you to shoot in lower light levels at lower ISO settings.

This isn't to say that you have to use the largest aperture on your lens. A good place to begin is f/5.6. This will give you enough depth of field to keep the entire face in focus, while providing enough blur to eliminate distractions in the background. This isn't a hard-and-fast setting; it's just a good all-around number to start with. Your aperture might change depending on the focal length of the lens you are using and on the amount of blur that you want for your foreground and background elements.

FIGURE 6.2
Using a wide aperture, especially with a longer lens, blurs distracting background details.

ISO 100
1/400 sec.
f/3.2
135mm lens

GO WIDE FOR ENVIRONMENTAL PORTRAITS

There will be times when your subject's environment is of great significance to the story you want to tell. This might mean using a smaller aperture to get more detail in the background or foreground. Once again, by using Av mode you can set your aperture to a higher f-stop, such as f/8 or f/11, and include the important details of the scene that surrounds your subject.

Using a wider-than-normal lens can also assist in getting more depth of field as well as showing the surrounding area. A wide-angle lens requires less stopping down of the aperture to achieve an acceptable depth of field. This is because wide-angle lenses cover a greater area, so the depth of field appears to cover a greater percentage of the scene.

A wider lens might also be necessary to relay more information about the scenery (**Figure 6.3**). Select a lens length that is wide enough to tell the story but not so wide that you distort the subject. There's nothing quite as unflattering as giving someone a big, distorted nose (unless you are going for that sort of look). When shooting a portrait with a wide-angle lens, keep the subject away from the edge of the frame. This will reduce the distortion, especially in very wide focal lengths. As the lens length increases, distortion will be reduced. I generally don't like to go wider than about 24mm for portraits. For standard portraits, I prefer a 55mm lens setting.

FIGURE 6.3
A wide-angle lens allows you to capture more of the environment in the scene without having to increase the distance between you and the subject.

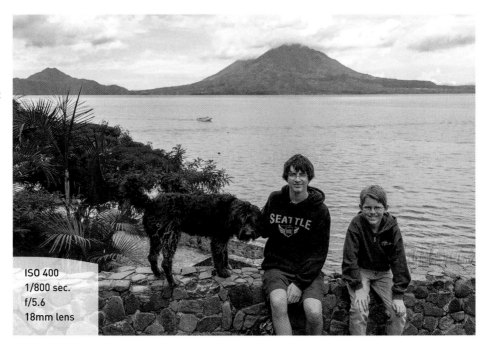

ISO 400
1/800 sec.
f/5.6
18mm lens

METERING BASICS

There are multiple metering modes in your camera, but the way they work is very similar. A light meter measures the amount of light being reflected off your subject and then renders a suggested exposure value based on the brightness of the subject and the ISO setting of the sensor. To establish this value, the meter averages all of the brightness values to come up with a middle tone, sometimes referred to as 18 percent gray. The exposure value is then rendered based on this middle-gray value. This means that a white wall would be underexposed and a black wall would be overexposed in an effort to make each one appear gray. To assist with special lighting situations, the T4i has four metering modes: Evaluative (**Figure 6.4**), which uses the entire frame; Partial (**Figure 6.5**), which uses the middle 9 percent of the frame; Spot (**Figure 6.6**), which takes specific readings from small areas (often used with a gray card); and Center-weighted (**Figure 6.7**), which looks at the entire frame but places most of the exposure emphasis on the center of the frame.

FIGURE 6.4
The Evaluative metering mode uses the entire frame.

FIGURE 6.5
The Partial metering mode uses the middle of the frame.

FIGURE 6.6
The Spot metering mode uses a very small area of the frame.

FIGURE 6.7
The Center-weighted metering mode looks at the entire frame but emphasizes the center of it.

METERING MODES FOR PORTRAITS

For most portrait situations, the Evaluative metering mode is ideal. (For more on how metering works, see the "Metering Basics" sidebar.) This mode measures light values from all portions of the viewfinder and then establishes a proper exposure for the scene. The only problem that you might encounter when using this metering mode is when you have very light or very dark backgrounds in your portrait shots.

In these instances, the meter might be fooled into using the wrong exposure information because it will be trying to lighten or darken the entire scene based on the prominence of dark or light areas (**Figure 6.8**). You can deal with this in one of two ways. You can use the Exposure Compensation feature, which we cover in Chapter 7, to dial in adjustments for over- and underexposure. Or you can change the metering mode from Evaluative to Partial or Center-weighted metering. The Partial metering mode uses only the center area of the viewfinder (about 9 percent) to get its exposure information. This is the best way to achieve proper exposure for most portraits; metering off of skin tones, averaged with hair and clothing, will often give a more accurate exposure (**Figure 6.9**). This metering mode is also great to use when the subject is strongly backlit.

FIGURE 6.8
(left) The light background color and clothing fooled the meter into choosing a slightly underexposed setting for the photo.

FIGURE 6.9
(right) When I switch to either the Partial or the Center-weighted metering mode, the camera will ignore much of the background and add a little more time to the exposure.

ISO 100
1/250 sec.
f/3.2
105mm lens

ISO 100
1/125 sec.
f/3.2
110mm lens

SETTING YOUR METERING MODE TO PARTIAL METERING

1. Press the Set button on the back of the camera to activate the Quick Control screen.

2. Move the selection to the Metering mode icon (**A**).

3. Use the Main dial to scroll through the metering modes until you find the symbol for Partial metering mode. The names of the different modes will appear near the bottom of the screen. If you press the Set button a second time, you can see all of the available metering modes (**B**).

4. Press the Set button to return to shooting mode.

A

B

USING THE AE LOCK FEATURE

There will often be times when your subject is not in the center of the frame but you still want to use the Partial metering mode. So how can you get an accurate reading if the subject isn't in the center? Try using the AE (Auto Exposure) Lock feature to hold the exposure setting while you recompose.

AE Lock lets you use the exposure setting from any portion of the scene that you think is appropriate, and then lock that setting in regardless of how the scene looks when you recompose. An example of this would be when you're shooting a photograph of someone and a large amount of blue sky appears in the picture. Normally, the meter might be fooled by all that bright sky and try to reduce the exposure. Using AE Lock, you can establish the correct metering by zooming in on the subject (or even pointing the camera toward the ground), taking the meter reading and locking it in with AE Lock, and then recomposing and taking your photo with the locked-in exposure.

SHOOTING WITH THE AE LOCK FEATURE

1. Find the AE Lock (✱) button on the back of the camera and place your thumb on it.

2. While looking through the viewfinder, place the center focus point on your subject.

3. Press and hold the AE Lock button to get a meter reading. A star will appear in your viewfinder, letting you know that the exposure has been locked.

4. Recompose your shot, and then take the photo.

5. To take more than one photo without having to take another meter reading, just hold down the AE Lock button until you are done using the meter setting.

FOCUSING: THE EYES HAVE IT

It has been said that the eyes are the windows to the soul, and nothing could be truer when you are taking a photograph of someone (**Figure 6.10**). You could have the perfect composition and exposure, but if the eyes aren't sharp, the entire image suffers. While there are many different focusing modes to choose from on your T4i, for portrait work you can't beat One Shot mode using a single focusing point. One Shot focusing will establish a single focus for the lens and then hold it until you take the photograph; the other focusing modes continue focusing until the photograph is taken. The single-point selection lets you place the focusing point right on your subject's eye and set that spot as the critical focus point. Using One Shot mode lets you get that focus and recompose all in one motion.

SETTING UP FOR ONE SHOT FOCUSING MODE

1. Press the right Cross key, the one labeled AF, on the back of your camera.

2. Rotate the Main dial or use the left/right Cross keys to change the focusing mode to One Shot, then press the Set button.

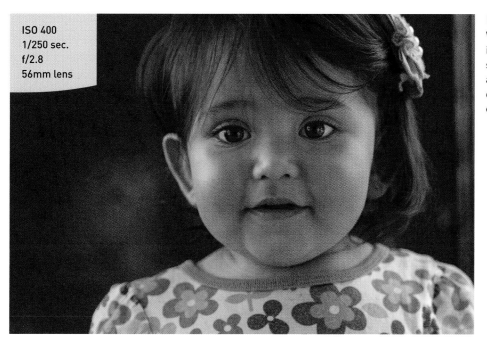

ISO 400
1/250 sec.
f/2.8
56mm lens

FIGURE 6.10
When photograph-
ing people, you
should almost
always place the
emphasis on the
eyes.

SETTING YOUR FOCUS TO A SINGLE POINT

1. Press the Focus Point Selection button (at the top right on the back of the camera) and then look in your viewfinder.

2. Rotate the Main dial, and watch the illuminated points change on the rear LCD (or in the viewfinder) as you move the dial. Select any single point from among the nine available points. If all of the points are lit up, that means you are in automatic focus point selection mode. Keep going until you have just the one point you want selected.

Now, to shoot using this focus point, place that point on your subject's eye, and press the shutter button halfway until the focus point flashes and you hear the chirp. While still holding the shutter button down halfway, recompose and take your shot.

I typically use the center point for focus selection. I find it easier to place that point directly on the location where my critical focus should be established and then recompose the shot. Even though the single point can be selected from any of the focus points, it typically takes longer to figure out where those points should be in relation to my subject. By using the center point, I can quickly establish focus and get on with my shooting.

CLASSIC BLACK AND WHITE PORTRAITS

There is something timeless about a black and white portrait. It eliminates the distraction of color and puts all the emphasis on the subject. To get great black and whites without having to resort to any image-processing software, set your picture style to Monochrome (**Figure 6.11**). You should know that the picture styles are automatically applied when shooting with the JPEG file format. If you are shooting in RAW, the picture that shows up on your rear LCD display will look black and white, but it will appear as a color image when you open it in your Digital Photo Professional software. You can use the software to apply the Monochrome picture style or any other style to your RAW image.

The real key to using the Monochrome picture style is to customize it for your portrait subject. The style can be changed to alter the sharpness and contrast. For women, children, puppies, and anyone else who should look somewhat soft, set the Sharpness setting to 0 or 1. For old cowboys, longshoremen, and anyone else you want to look really detailed, try a setting of 6 or 7. I like to leave Contrast at a setting of around –1 or –2. This gives me a nice range of tones throughout the image.

The other adjustment that you should try is to change the picture style's Filter effect from None to one of the four available settings (Yellow, Orange, Red, and Green). Using the filters will have the effect of either lightening or darkening the skin tones. The Red and Yellow filters usually lighten skin, while the Green filter can make skin appear a bit darker. Experiment to see which one works best for your subject.

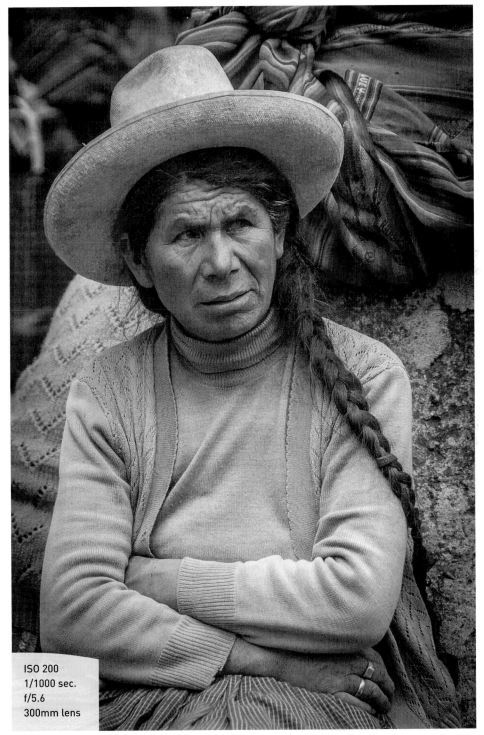

FIGURE 6.11
Getting high-quality
black and white
portraits is as
simple as setting
the picture style to
Monochrome.

ISO 200
1/1000 sec.
f/5.6
300mm lens

SETTING YOUR PICTURE STYLE TO MONOCHROME

1. Start by pressing the Menu button.

2. Use the Main dial to scroll to the second camera shooting menu (second from the left).

3. Using the Cross keys, highlight the Picture Style setting and press the Set button (**A**).

4. Use the down Cross key to highlight the Monochrome setting, and lock it in by pressing the Set button again (**B**).

A

B

Your camera will continue to shoot with the Monochrome picture style until you change it to another setting.

CUSTOMIZING THE PICTURE STYLE SETTINGS

1. When you're in the Picture Style section of the menu where you have Monochrome selected, press the Info button located to the left of your viewfinder.

2. Use the up/down Cross keys to highlight the setting you would like to change and press the Set button.

3. Now use the left/right Cross keys to move the cursor to a new position on the scale (the default setting will remain marked with a gray arrow) or to select a different filter, and press the Set button (**C, D**).

4. Perform the same process for the other options, then press the Menu button to return to the regular menu screen. You can now start shooting with your new settings.

C

D

THE PORTRAIT PICTURE STYLE FOR BETTER SKIN TONES

As long as we are talking about picture styles for portraits, there is another style on your T4i that has been tuned specifically for this type of shooting. Oddly enough, it's called Portrait. To set this style on your camera, simply follow the same directions as earlier, except this time select the Portrait style instead of Monochrome. There are also individual options for the Portrait style that, like the Monochrome style, include sharpness and contrast. You can also change the saturation (how intense the colors will be) and the color tone, which lets you change the skin tones from more reddish to more yellowish. I prefer brighter colors, so I like to boost the Saturation setting to +2 and leave everything else at the defaults. You won't be able to use the same adjustments for everyone, especially when it comes to color tone, so do some experimenting to see what works best.

DETECT FACES WITH LIVE VIEW

Face detection in digital cameras has been around for a few years, but it's still a new concept in the world of the DSLR. Your T4i has three different autofocus modes for Live View: Quick, Live, and my personal favorite, Face Detection. These modes are different from the standard modes like One Shot, AI Servo, and AI Focus. Face Detection mode is probably the slowest of the Live View focusing modes, so I use it mostly when I am working with a tripod or when my subjects are going to remain fairly still. When you turn on Live View with Face Detection focusing, the camera does an amazing thing: it zeroes in on any face appearing on the LCD and places a box around it (**Figure 6.12**). I'm not sure how it works; it just does.

If there is more than one face in the frame, the box will appear over just one of them, but it will have little arrows to the side of it. Just press the Cross keys from side to side to make the box jump from one face to the other until you have selected the one that you want to focus on.

Manual Callout

There is a complete chapter in your manual that is dedicated to using Live View mode. It can be found on pages 143–166.

FIGURE 6.12

The Live View Face Detection mode can lock in on your subject's face for easy focusing.

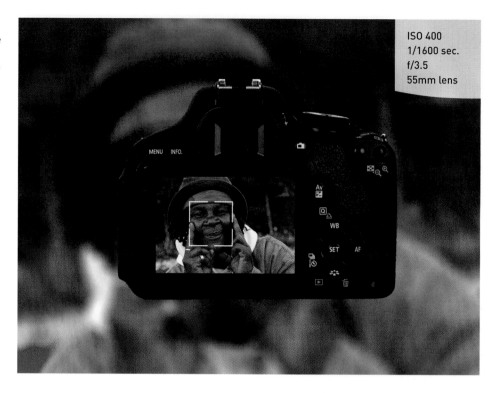

ISO 400
1/1600 sec.
f/3.5
55mm lens

SETTING UP AND SHOOTING WITH LIVE VIEW AND FACE DETECTION FOCUSING

1. Press the Menu button and use the Main dial to highlight the fourth shooting menu screen. Then highlight the Live View shoot option and make sure it is set to Enable.

2. Press the Menu button to exit the menu mode and get ready for shooting.

3. Activate the Live View function by pressing the Live View button located on the back of the camera, to the right of the viewfinder.

4. Point your camera at a person and watch as the frame appears over the face in the LCD.

5. Press and hold the shutter release button halfway to focus on the face, and wait until you hear the confirmation chirp.

6. Press the shutter button fully to take the photograph.

If you are having difficulty getting a face in focus, you can press the Q button (for the Quick Control screen) to activate the Live View options and make sure the AF option is highlighted. Then just use the Main dial to switch from the Face Detection focusing mode to AF Live mode (**Figure 6.13**). This will bring up a focus point in the center of the screen that you can toggle to a new location.

FIGURE 6.13
Change the focus mode if you can't get the camera to detect any faces.

USING LIVE VIEW'S GRID OVERLAY

There is another benefit to using Live View: the grid overlay. This is a feature that actually places a grid over your image, dividing it into thirds, which can be of great benefit in properly composing your image.

SETTING UP LIVE VIEW'S GRID OPTION

1. Press the Menu button and then use the Main dial to get to the fourth shooting menu screen.
2. Using the Cross keys, scroll down to Grid display and press Set (**A**).
3. Scroll down to Grid display, press Set, and then choose Grid 1 (**B**).

A

B

Now when you activate Live View, you will see the one-third grid overlay superimposed on the rear display (**Figure 6.14**). This effect shows up only on the display and will not be visible in your final image.

FIGURE 6.14
Using Live View's Grid option can help you compose your shots.

USE FILL FLASH FOR REDUCING SHADOWS

A common problem when taking pictures of people outside, especially during the midday hours, is that the overhead sun can create dark shadows under the eyes and chin. You could have your subject turn his or her face to the sun, but that is usually considered cruel and unusual punishment. So how can you have your subject's back to the sun and still get a decent exposure of the face? Try turning on your flash to fill in the shadows. This also works well when you are photographing someone who's wearing a baseball cap or someone who has a bright scene behind them (**Figure 6.15**). The fill flash helps lighten the subject so they don't appear in shadow, while providing a really nice catchlight in the eyes.

The key to using the flash as a fill is to not use it on full power. If you do, the camera will try to balance the flash with the daylight, and you will get a very flat and featureless face.

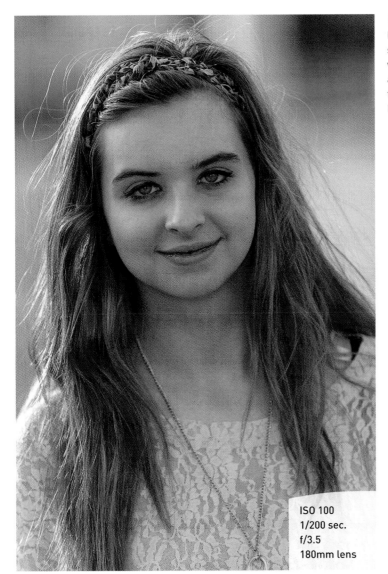

ISO 100
1/200 sec.
f/3.5
180mm lens

CATCHLIGHT

A *catchlight* is that little sparkle that adds life to the eyes. When you are photographing a person with a light source in front of them, you will usually get a reflection of that light in the eye, be it your flash, the sun, or something else brightly reflecting in the eye. The light is reflected off the surface of the eyes as bright highlights, which brings attention to the eyes.

SETTING UP AND SHOOTING WITH FILL FLASH

1. Press the pop-up flash button to raise your pop-up flash into the ready position.

2. Press the Q button to activate the Quick Control screen.

3. Use the Cross keys to position the cursor over the Flash exposure comp option.

4. Use the Main dial to select the desired amount of flash compensation.

5. Lightly press the shutter release button to exit the Quick Control screen.

One problem that can quickly surface when using the on-camera flash is red-eye. Not to worry, though—we will talk about that in Chapter 8.

PEOPLE ON THE MOVE

Not all portraits are shot with the subject sitting in a chair, posed and ready for the picture. Sometimes you might want to get an action shot that says something about the person, similar to an environmental portrait. Children, especially, just like to move. Why fight it? Set up an action portrait instead.

For the photo in **Figure 6.16**, I set my camera to Shutter Priority mode. I knew that there would be a good deal of movement involved, and I wanted to make sure that I had a fairly high shutter speed to freeze the action, so I set it to 1/125 of a second. I used a continuous focus mode, set the drive mode to Continuous, and just started firing off shots as he moved within range. There were quite a few throwaway shots, but I was able to capture one that captured him in the midst of casting the net.

ISO 400
1/800 sec.
f/5.6
220mm lens

FIGURE 6.16
Although I prefer to shoot my people shots in Aperture Priority mode, the key to this shot was using Shutter Priority mode.

TIPS FOR SHOOTING BETTER PORTRAITS

Before we get to the assignments for this chapter, I thought it might be a good idea to leave you with a few extra portrait pointers that don't necessarily have anything specific to do with your camera. There are entire books that cover things like portrait lighting, posing, and so on, but here are a few pointers that will make your people pics look a lot better.

AVOID THE CENTER OF THE FRAME

This falls under the category of composition. Place your subject to the side of the frame (**Figure 6.17**)—it just looks more interesting than plunking them smack dab in the middle (**Figure 6.18**).

ISO 400
1/100 sec.
f/5.6
120mm lens

ISO 400
1/80 sec.
f/5.6
120mm lens

CHOOSE THE RIGHT LENS

Choosing the correct lens can make a huge impact on your portraits. A wide-angle lens can distort the features of your subject, which can lead to an unflattering portrait (**Figure 6.19**). Select a longer focal length if you will be close to your subject (**Figure 6.20**).

ISO 100
1/160 sec.
f/3.2
24mm lens

ISO 100
1/125 sec.
f/3.2
70mm lens

FIGURE 6.19
(left) At this close distance, the 24mm lens is distorting the subject's face.

FIGURE 6.20
(right) By zooming out to 70mm, I am able to remove the distortion for a much better photo.

DON'T CUT THEM OFF AT THE KNEES

There is an old rule about photographing people: never crop the picture at a joint. This means no cropping at the ankles or the knees. If you need to crop at the legs, the proper place to crop is mid-shin or mid-thigh (**Figure 6.21**).

USE THE FRAME

Have you ever noticed that most people are taller than they are wide? Turn your camera vertically for a more pleasing composition (**Figure 6.22**).

FIGURE 6.21
A good crop for people is at mid-thigh or mid-shin.

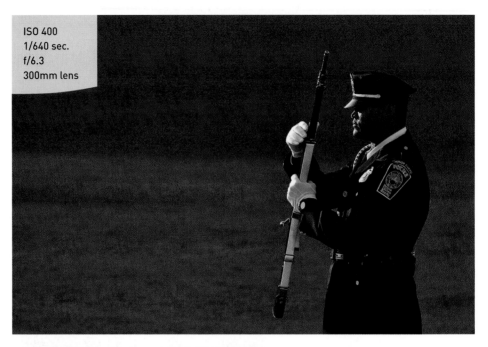

ISO 400
1/640 sec.
f/6.3
300mm lens

ISO 400
1/400 sec.
f/5.6
55mm lens

FIGURE 6.22
Get in the habit of turning your camera to a vertical position when shooting portraits. This is also referred to as portrait orientation.

SUNBLOCK FOR PORTRAITS

The midday sun can be harsh and can do unflattering things to people's faces (**Figure 6.23**). If you can, find a shady spot out of the direct sunlight. You will get softer shadows, smoother skin tones, and better detail (**Figure 6.24**). This holds true for overcast skies as well. Just be sure to adjust your white balance accordingly.

ISO 100
1/800 sec.
f/3.2
180mm lens

ISO 100
1/640 sec.
f/3.2
180mm lens

FIGURE 6.23
The bright, direct sunlight looks too harsh on the subject's face.

FIGURE 6.24
By moving her over just a couple of feet, I was able to get her out of the direct sun and into a much more flattering situation.

FRAME THE SCENE

Using elements in the scene to create a frame around your subject is a great way to draw the viewer in. You don't have to use a window frame to do this. Just look for elements in the foreground that could be used to force the viewer's eye toward your subject (**Figure 6.25**).

FIGURE 6.25
The bright railings help to create a great frame around the subject.

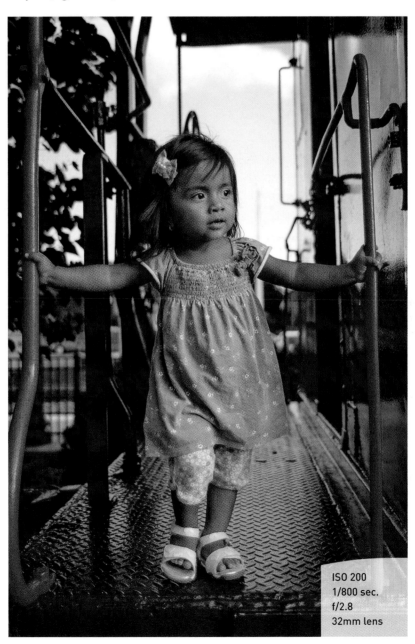

ISO 200
1/800 sec.
f/2.8
32mm lens

GET DOWN ON THEIR LEVEL

If you want better pictures of children, don't shoot from an adult's eye level. Getting the camera down to the child's level will make your images look more personal (**Figure 6.26**).

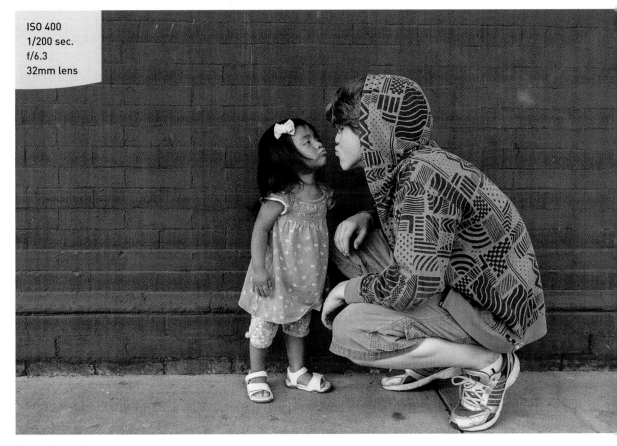

ISO 400
1/200 sec.
f/6.3
32mm lens

FIGURE 6.26
Whenever you are taking photographs of children, get your camera down on their level for a less imposing view.

DON'T BE AFRAID TO GET CLOSE

When you are taking someone's picture, don't be afraid of getting close and filling the frame (**Figure 6.27**). This doesn't mean you have to shoot from a foot away—try zooming in to capture the details.

TRY A LONG LENS FOR CANDID SHOTS

Putting a camera in someone's face can elicit some unnatural results. People just feel a need to pose, or they get nervous and stiff. If you really want to capture some nice portraits with a more candid feel, try shooting with a long lens (**Figure 6.28**). The distance will remove you and your camera from the equation, and people will tend to react more normally. If you are looking to be a street photographer, a long lens will be one of your best tools.

ISO 400
1/160 sec.
f/5.6
120mm lens

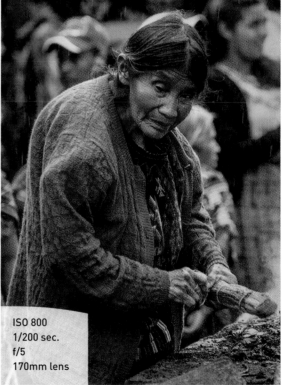

ISO 800
1/200 sec.
f/5
170mm lens

FIGURE 6.27
Filling the frame with the subject's face can lead to a much more intimate portrait.

FIGURE 6.28
Using a long lens can help you get more candid shots.

Chapter 6 Assignments

Depth of field in portraits

Let's start with something simple. Grab your favorite person and start experimenting with using different aperture settings. Shoot wide open (the widest your lens goes, such as f/2.8 or f/4) and then really stopped down (like f/22). Look at the difference in the depth of field and how it plays an important role in placing the attention on your subject. (Make sure you don't have your subject standing against the background. Give some distance so that there is a good blurring effect of the background at the wide f-stop setting.)

Discovering the qualities of natural light

Pick a nice sunny day and try shooting some portraits in the midday sun. If your subject is willing, have them turn so the sun is in their face. If they are still speaking to you after blinding them, have them turn their back to the sun. Try this with and without the fill flash so you can see the difference. Finally, move them into a completely shaded spot and take a few more.

Picking the right metering method

Find a very dark or light background and place your subject in front of it. Now take a couple of shots, giving a lot of space around your subject for the background to show. Now switch metering modes and use the AE Lock feature to get a more accurate reading of your subject. Notice the differences in exposure between the metering methods.

Picture styles for portraits

Have some fun playing with the different picture styles. Try the Portrait style as compared to the Standard style. Then try out Monochrome and play with the different color filter options to see how they affect skin tones.

Share your results with the book's Flickr group!

Join the group here: flickr.com/groups/t4i650dfromsnapshotstogreatshots

7

ISO 800
1/80 sec.
f/6.3
135mm lens

Landscape Photography

TIPS, TOOLS, AND TECHNIQUES TO GET THE MOST OUT OF YOUR LANDSCAPE PHOTOGRAPHY

There has always been something about shooting landscapes that has brought a sense of joy to my photography. It might have something to do with being outdoors and working at the mercy of Mother Nature. Maybe it's the way it challenges me to visualize the landscape and try to capture it with my camera. It truly is a celebration of light, composition, and the world we live in.

In this chapter, we will explore some of the features of the T4i that not only improve the look of your landscape photography but also make it easier to take great shots. We will also explore some typical scenarios and discuss methods to bring out the best in your landscape work.

PORING OVER THE PICTURE

Whenever I travel, I try to do a little research before I leave to see if there are any interesting photo locations in the area that I will be traveling to. I'm not always on a photography trip, but I like to have some options if I find some free time. This was the case on my last trip to Portland, Oregon. Luckily, it's an area that is full of fantastic landscapes, like this waterfall in the Columbia River Gorge area.

The Landscape picture style makes the colors pop.

A low ISO helped to increase the length of the shutter speed.

To lengthen my exposure time,
I selected a small aperture.

The flow of the water was
accentuated by using a
long shutter speed.

ISO 100
1/10 sec.
f/6.3
19mm lens

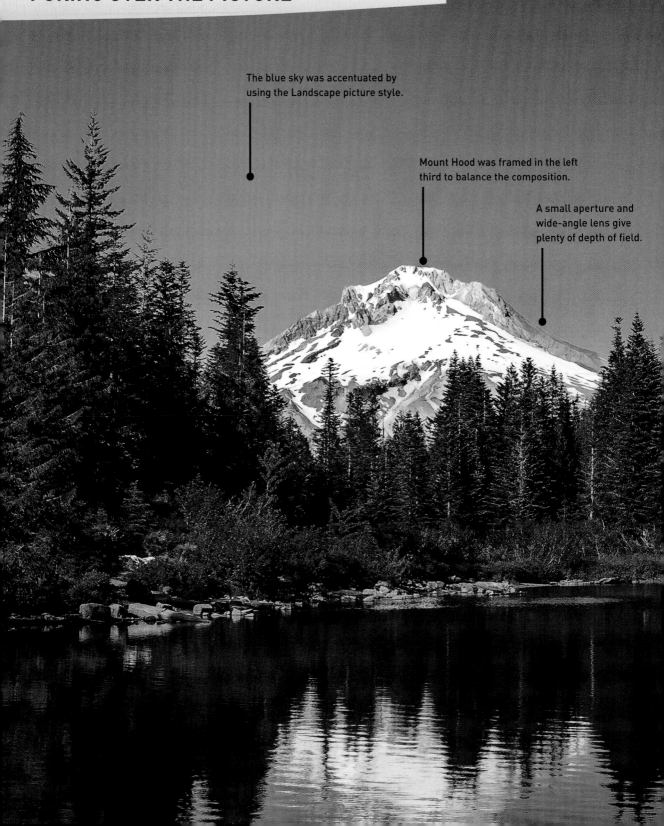

The blue sky was accentuated by using the Landscape picture style.

Mount Hood was framed in the left third to balance the composition.

A small aperture and wide-angle lens give plenty of depth of field.

This is another shot from my trip to Portland. This one was taken from a spot called Mirror Lake, which required an hour-and-a-half hike up a mountain trail to reach. I didn't realize at the time just how much work it would be to get there, but sometimes the hard work is rewarded with a scene like this.

I used a tripod so that my image would be extremely sharp.

ISO 100
1/60 sec.
f/14
35mm lens

SHARP AND IN FOCUS: USING TRIPODS

Throughout the previous chapters, we have concentrated on using the camera to create great images. We will continue that trend through this chapter, but there is one additional piece of equipment that is crucial in the world of landscape shooting: the tripod. Tripods are critical to your landscape work for a couple of reasons. The first relates to the time of day that you will be working. For reasons that will be explained later, the best light for most landscape work happens at sunrise and just before sunset. While this is the best time to shoot, it's also kind of dark. That means you'll be working with slow shutter speeds. Slow shutter speeds mean camera shake. Camera shake equals bad photos.

The second reason is also related to the amount of light that you're gathering with your camera. When taking landscape photos, you will usually want to be working with very small apertures, as they give you lots of depth of field. This also means that, once again, you will be working with slower-than-normal shutter speeds.

Slow shutter = camera shake = bad photos.

Do you see the pattern here? The one tool in your arsenal to truly defeat the camera shake issue and ensure tack-sharp photos is a good tripod (**Figure 7.1**).

FIGURE 7.1
A sturdy tripod is the key to sharp landscape photos.
(Photo: Scott Kelby)

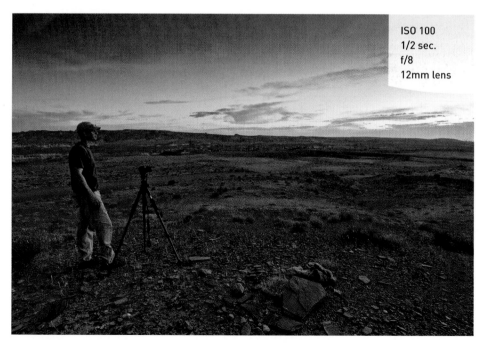

ISO 100
1/2 sec.
f/8
12mm lens

So what should you look for in a tripod? Well, first make sure it is sturdy enough to support your camera and any lens that you might want to use. Next, check the height of the tripod. Your day will end much better if you haven't been bent over all day to look through your viewfinder. Finally, think about getting a tripod that utilizes a quick-release head. This usually employs a plate that screws into the bottom of the camera and then quickly snaps into place on the tripod. This will be especially handy if you are going to move between shooting by hand and using the tripod. You can find more info on tripods in the bonus chapter "Pimp My Ride."

TRIPOD STABILITY

Most tripods have a center column that allows the user to extend the height of the camera above the point where the tripod legs join together. This might seem like a great idea, but the reality is that the higher you raise that column, the less stable your tripod becomes. Think of a tall building that sways near the top. To get the most solid base for your camera, always try to use it with the center column at its lowest point so that your camera is right at the apex of the tripod legs.

IS LENSES AND TRIPODS DON'T MIX

If you are using image stabilization (IS) lenses on your camera, remember to turn this feature off when you use a tripod (**Figure 7.2**). This is because the image stabilization can, while trying to minimize camera movement, actually *create* movement when the camera is already stable. To turn off the IS feature, just slide the Stabilizer selector switch on the side of the lens to the Off position.

FIGURE 7.2
Turn off the image stabilization feature when using a tripod.

SELECTING THE PROPER ISO

When you're shooting most landscape scenes, the ISO is the one factor that should only be changed as a last resort. While it is easy to select a higher ISO to get a smaller aperture, the noise that it can introduce into your images can be quite harmful (**Figures 7.3** and **7.4**). The noise not only can be visible as large grainy artifacts but can also be multicolored, which further degrades the image quality. Take a look at the image in Figure 7.4, which was taken with an ISO of 1600. The purpose was to shorten the shutter speed and still use a small aperture setting of f/22. The problem is that the noise level is so high that, in addition to being distracting, it is obscuring fine details in the canyon wall.

FIGURE 7.3
(left) A high ISO setting created a lot of digital noise in the shadows.

FIGURE 7.4
(right) When the image is enlarged, the noise is even more apparent.

ISO 1600
2 sec.
f/22
24mm lens

Now check out another image that was taken in the same canyon light but with a much lower ISO setting (**Figures 7.5** and **7.6**). As you can see, the noise levels are much lower, which means that my blacks look black, and the fine details are beautifully captured.

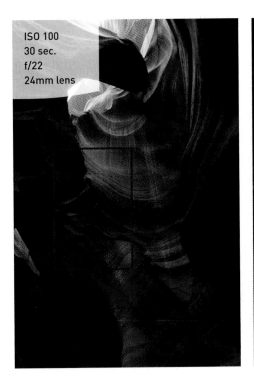

ISO 100
30 sec.
f/22
24mm lens

FIGURE 7.5
(left) By lowering the ISO to 100, I was able to avoid the noise and capture a clean image.

FIGURE 7.6
(right) Zooming in shows that the noise levels for this image are almost nonexistent.

When shooting landscapes, set your ISO to the lowest-possible setting at all times. Between the use of image stabilization lenses (if you are shooting handheld) and a good tripod, there should be few circumstances where you would need to shoot landscapes with anything above an ISO of 400.

USING NOISE REDUCTION

Both canyon images were taken with a tripod, but the image set to an ISO of 100 required four more stops of shutter speed (30 seconds at ISO 100) than the high ISO image (2 seconds at ISO 1600). The temptation to use higher ISOs should always be avoided, as the end result will be more image noise and less detail.

There can be an issue when using a low ISO setting: the sometimes-lengthy shutter speeds can also introduce noise. This noise is a result of the heating of the camera sensor as it is being exposed to light. This effect is not visible in short exposures, but as you start shooting with shutter speeds that exceed 1 second, the level of image noise can increase. Your camera has a couple of features that you can turn on to combat noise from long exposures and high ISOs.

SETTING UP NOISE REDUCTION

1. Press the Menu button, use the Main dial to get to the third shooting menu, highlight the High ISO speed NR selection, and press Set (**A**).

2. The default setting is Standard, but you may require the Strong setting for really high ISOs (**B**).

3. Press the Menu button to return to the shooting menu, and then select Long exp. noise reduction. Press the Set button to change the options (**C**).

4. The default setting is Auto, which will handle most scenarios. If you know you are going to be making extremely long exposures, you should probably go ahead and set it to On (**D**).

A

B

C

D

SELECTING A WHITE BALANCE

This probably seems like a no-brainer. If it's sunny, select Daylight; if it's overcast, choose the Shade or Cloudy setting. Those choices wouldn't be wrong for those circumstances, but why limit yourself? Sometimes you can change the mood of the photo by selecting a white balance that doesn't quite fit the light for the scene that you are shooting. **Figure 7.7** is an example of a correct white balance. It was late afternoon and the sun was starting to move low in the sky, giving everything that warm afternoon glow. The white balance for this image was set to Daylight. But what if I want to make the scene look like it had been shot in the early morning hours? Simple—I just change the white balance to Fluorescent, which is a much cooler setting (**Figure 7.8**).

ISO 1250
1/400 sec.
f/8
95mm lens

FIGURE 7.7
Using the "proper" white balance yields predictable results.

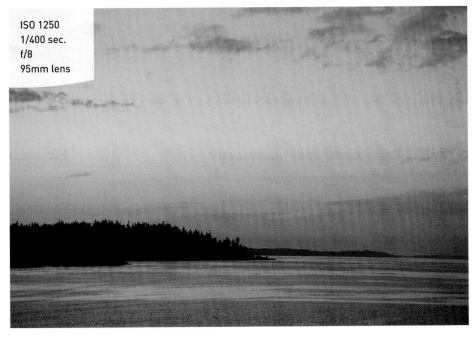

ISO 1250
1/400 sec.
f/8
95mm lens

FIGURE 7.8
Changing the white balance to Fluorescent gives the impression that the picture was taken at a different time of day than it really was.

You can select the most appropriate white balance for your shooting conditions in a couple of ways. The first is to just take a shot, review it on the LCD, and keep the one you like. Of course, you would need to take one for each white balance setting, which means that you will have to take about seven different shots to see which is most pleasing. The second method, and my personal favorite, doesn't require taking a single shot. Instead, it uses Live View to get perfectly selected white balances. Live View gives instant feedback as you scroll through all of the white balance settings and displays them for you right on the LCD. Even better, you can choose a custom setting that will let you dial in exactly the right look for your image. (See Chapter 6 for more on Live View.)

USING LIVE VIEW TO PREVIEW DIFFERENT WHITE BALANCE SETTINGS

1. Press the Live View button located to the right of the rear LCD screen.
2. With Live View activated, press the Q button, which will bring up the Live View options on the sides of the screen.
3. Use the up/down Cross keys to highlight the White Balance icon (the top one on the right side of the screen), and then rotate the Main dial or press the left/right Cross keys to change the white balance.
4. Select the white balance setting that looks most appropriate for your scene, then press the Q button to lock in your change and resume shooting.
5. Press the Live View button once again to exit Live View mode.

USING THE LANDSCAPE PICTURE STYLE

When shooting landscapes, I always look for great color and contrast. This is one of the reasons that so many landscape shots are taken in the early morning or during sunset. The light is much more vibrant and colorful at these times of day and adds a sense of drama to an image. You can help boost this effect, especially in the less-than-golden hours of the day, by using the Landscape picture style (**Figures 7.9** and **7.10**). Just as in the Landscape mode found in the Basic zone, you can set up your landscape shooting so that you capture images with increased sharpness and a slight boost in blues and greens. This style will add some pop to your landscapes without the need for additional processing in any software.

ISO 400
1/125 sec.
f/10
18mm lens

FIGURE 7.9
Using the Standard picture style, the colors are OK but don't really pop.

ISO 400
1/125 sec.
f/10
18mm lens

FIGURE 7.10
The Landscape picture style adds sharpness, a little contrast, and more vivid color to skies and vegetation.

SETTING UP THE LANDSCAPE PICTURE STYLE

1. Press the Menu button, then rotate the Main dial to the second shooting menu.

2. Use the Cross keys to navigate down the menu list until you get to Picture Style, then press the Set button (**A**).

3. Use the down Cross key to highlight the Landscape setting, and then press the Set button to lock in your change (**B**).

A

B

If you are shooting RAW, your images will look like they have the picture style applied when you view them on the back of the camera, but the style will go away once you open the images in post-processing software. You will need to add the picture style back as part of your post-processing. Only JPEGs have the picture style applied as part of the final in-camera image processing.

TAMING BRIGHT SKIES WITH EXPOSURE COMPENSATION

Balancing exposure in scenes that have a wide contrast in tonal ranges can be extremely challenging. The one thing you should try not to do is overexpose your skies to the point of blowing out your highlights (unless, of course, that is the look you are going for). It's one thing to have white clouds, but it's a completely different and bad thing to have no detail at all in those clouds. This usually happens when the camera is trying to gain exposure in the darker areas of the image (**Figure 7.11**).

The one way to tell if you have blown out your highlights is to check the Highlight Alert, or "blinkies," feature on your camera (see the "How I Shoot" section in Chapter 4). When you take a shot where the highlights are exposed beyond the point of having any detail, that area will blink in your LCD display. It is up to you to determine if that particular area is important enough to regain detail by altering your exposure. If the answer is yes, then the easiest way to go about it is to use some exposure compensation.

ISO 400
1/400 sec.
f/5.6
49mm lens

FIGURE 7.11
The camera has done a good job of exposing the foreground, but the sky is too light and lacks detail.

With this feature, you can force your camera to choose an exposure that ranges, in 1/3-stop increments, from five stops over to five stops under the metered exposure (**Figure 7.12**).

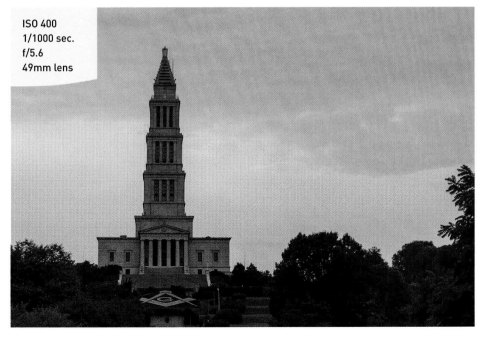

ISO 400
1/1000 sec.
f/5.6
49mm lens

FIGURE 7.12
A compensation of 1 1/3 stops of underexposure gave me the darker, more colorful skies that I was after.

USING EXPOSURE COMPENSATION TO REGAIN DETAIL IN HIGHLIGHTS

1. Activate the camera meter by lightly pressing the shutter release button.

2. Press and hold the Av button.

3. Use the Main dial to set the amount of over- or underexposure that you desire.

4. Take another photo.

5. If the blinkies are gone, you are good to go. If not, keep subtracting from your exposure by 1/3 of a stop until you have a good exposure in the highlights.

I generally keep my camera set to −1/3 stop for most of my landscape work unless I am working with a location that is very dark or low key.

HIGH-KEY AND LOW-KEY IMAGES

When you hear someone refer to a subject as being *high key*, it usually means that the entire image is composed of a very bright subject with very few shadow areas—think snow or beach. It makes sense, then, that a *low-key* subject has very few highlight areas and a predominance of shadow areas. Think of a cityscape at night as an example of a low-key photo.

SHOOTING BEAUTIFUL BLACK AND WHITE LANDSCAPES

There is nothing as timeless as a beautiful black and white landscape photo. For many, it is the purest form of photography. The genre conjures up thoughts of Ansel Adams out in Yosemite Valley, capturing stunning monoliths with his 8x10 view camera. Well, just because you are shooting with a digital camera doesn't mean you can't create your own stunning photos using the power of the Monochrome picture style. (See the "Classic Black and White Portraits" section of Chapter 6 for instructions on setting up this feature.) Not only can you shoot in black and white, you can also apply built-in filters to lighten or darken different elements within your scene, as well as add contrast and definition.

The four filter colors are yellow, orange, red, and green. The most typically used filters in black and white photography are red and yellow. This is because the color of the filter will darken opposite colors and lighten similar colors. So if you want to darken a blue sky, you would use a yellow filter because blue is the opposite of yellow. To darken green foliage, you would use a red filter. Check out the series of shots in **Figure 7.13** with different filters applied.

ISO 400
1/500 sec.
f/11
40mm lens

FIGURE 7.13
Adding color filter settings to the Monochrome picture style allows you to brighten or darken elements in your scene. The top-right image has no filter applied to it. The bottom-left has a green filter, and the bottom-right has a red filter.

You can see that there is no real difference in contrast between the color image and the black and white image with no filter. The green filter has the effect of darkening the sky a little and giving a lighter look to the vegetation. Using the red filter makes the sky and the vegetation darker. For this particular shot, I much prefer the look of the green filter.

Other options in the Monochrome picture style enable you to adjust the sharpness and contrast and even add some color toning to the final image. This information is also in the "Classic Black and White Portraits" section of Chapter 6. I like to have Sharpness set to 5 and Contrast set to 1 for my landscape images. This gives an overall look to the black and white image that is reminiscent of the classic black and white films. Experiment with the various settings to find the combination that is most pleasing to you.

THE GOLDEN LIGHT

If you ask any professional landscape photographer what their favorite time of day to shoot is, chances are they will tell you it's the hours surrounding daybreak and sunset (**Figures 7.14** and **7.15**). The reason for this is that the light is coming from a very low angle to the landscape, which creates shadows and gives depth and character. There is also a quality to the light that seems cleaner and is more colorful than the light you get when shooting at midday. One thing that can dramatically improve any morning or evening shot is the presence of clouds. The sun will fill the underside of the clouds with a palette of colors and add drama to your skies.

FIGURE 7.14
The right subject can come alive with color during the first few minutes of sunrise.

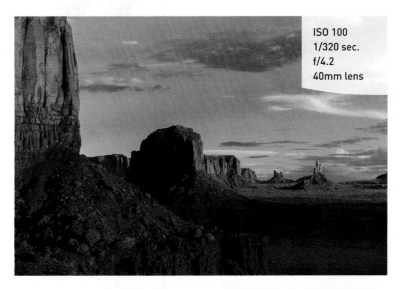

ISO 100
1/320 sec.
f/4.2
40mm lens

FIGURE 7.15
Late afternoon sun is usually warmer and adds drama and warmth to the subject.

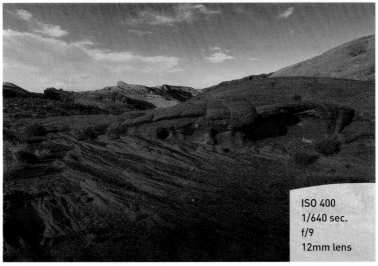

ISO 400
1/640 sec.
f/9
12mm lens

WHERE TO FOCUS

Large landscape scenes are fun to photograph, but they can present a problem: where exactly do you focus when you want everything to be sharp? Since our goal is to create a great landscape photo, we need to concentrate on creating an image that is tack sharp, with a depth of field that renders great focus throughout the scene.

I have already stressed the importance of a good tripod when shooting landscapes. The tripod lets you concentrate on the aperture portion of the exposure without worrying about how long your shutter will be open. This is because the tripod provides the stability to handle any shutter speed you might need when shooting at small apertures. I find that for most of my landscape work I set my camera to Aperture Priority mode and the ISO to 100 (for a clean, noise-free image).

However, shooting with the smallest aperture on your lens doesn't necessarily mean that you will get the proper sharpness throughout your image. The real key is knowing where in the scene to focus your lens to maximize the depth of field for your chosen aperture. To do this, you must utilize something called the "hyper focal distance" of your lens.

Hyper focal distance, also referred to as HFD, is the point of focus that will give you the greatest acceptable sharpness from a point near your camera all the way out to infinity. If you combine good HFD practice with a small aperture, you will get images that are sharp to infinity.

There are a couple of ways to do this, and the one that is probably the easiest is, as you might guess, the one that is most widely used by working pros. When you have your shot all set up and composed, focus on an object that is about one-third of the distance into your frame (**Figure 7.16**). It is usually pretty close to the proper distance and will render favorable results. When you have the focus set, use your Depth of Field Preview button to check the sharpness of all the objects in your scene. The button is located just under the lens release button and is activated once you have depressed the shutter button partway (**Figure 7.17**).

FIGURE 7.16

To get maximum focus from near to far, the focus was set one-third of the way into the image, on the ridge of trees in the lower-left. I then recomposed before taking the picture. Using this point of focus with an aperture of f/16 gave me a sharply focused image, from the trees to the distant mountains.

ISO 400
1/400 sec.
f/16
40mm lens

FIGURE 7.17

Using the Depth of Field Preview button can help ensure that the image is sharp.

TACK SHARP

Here's one of those terms that photographers like to throw around. *Tack sharp* refers not only to the focus of an image but also to the overall sharpness of the image. This usually means that there is excellent depth of field in terms of sharp focus for all elements in the image. It also means that there is no sign of camera shake, which can give soft edges to subjects that should look nice and crisp. To get your images tack sharp, use a small depth of field, don't forget your tripod, use the self-timer to activate the shutter if no cable release is handy, and practice achieving good hyper focal distance when picking your point of focus.

When the Depth of Field Preview button is depressed, it will cause the lens to close down to the selected aperture and let you preview the depth of field directly through your viewfinder. You can also use this feature during Live View mode to see the depth of field directly on your LCD display.

One thing to remember is that as your lens gets wider in focal length, your HFD will be closer to the camera position. This is because the wider the lens, the greater the depth of field you can achieve. This is yet another reason why a good wide-angle lens is indispensable to the landscape shooter.

EASIER FOCUSING

There's no denying that the automatic focus features on the T4i are great, but sometimes it just pays to turn them off and go manual. This is especially true if you are shooting on a tripod: once you have your shot composed in the viewfinder and you are ready to focus, chances are that the area you want to focus on is not going to be in the area of one of the focus points. Often this is the case when you have a foreground element that is fairly low in the frame. You could use a single focus point set low in your viewfinder and then pan the camera down until it rests on your subject. But then you would have to press the shutter button halfway to focus the camera and then try to recompose and lock down the tripod. It's no easy task.

But you can have the best of both worlds by having the camera focus for you, then switching to manual focus to comfortably recompose your shot (**Figure 7.18**).

GETTING FOCUSED WHILE USING A TRIPOD

1. Set up your shot and find the area that you want to focus on.
2. Pan your tripod head so that your active focus point is on that spot.
3. Press the shutter button halfway to focus the camera, and then remove your finger from the button.
4. Switch the camera to manual focus by sliding the switch on the lens barrel from AF to MF.
5. Recompose the composition on the tripod and then take the shot.

The camera will fire without trying to refocus the lens. This works especially well for wide-angle lenses, which can be difficult to focus in manual mode.

FIGURE 7.18

Using the hyper focal distance (HFD) one-third rule, I focused on the rock in the lower portion of the image, then switched the lens to manual focus before recomposing for the final shot.

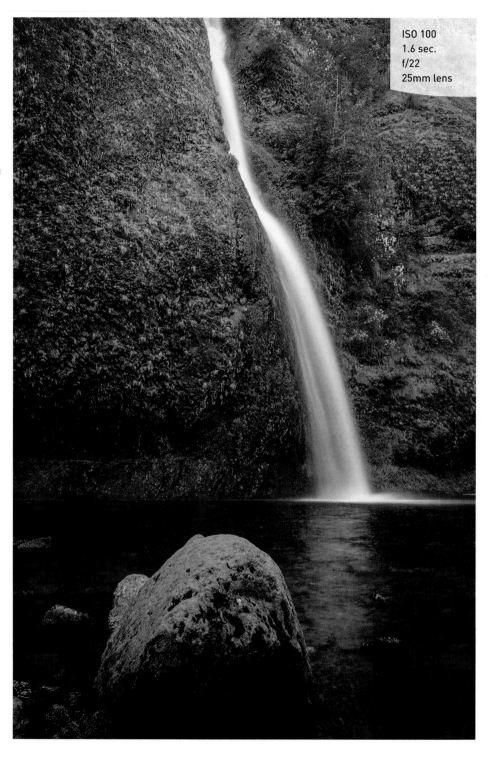

ISO 100
1.6 sec.
f/22
25mm lens

MAKING WATER FLUID

There's nothing quite as satisfying for the landscape shooter as capturing a silky waterfall shot. Creating the smooth-flowing effect is as simple as adjusting your shutter speed to allow the water to be in motion while the shutter is open. The key is to have your camera on a stable platform (such as a tripod) so that you can use a shutter speed that's long enough to work (**Figure 7.19**). To achieve a great effect, use a shutter speed that is at least 1/15 of a second or longer.

ISO 100
1.3 sec.
f/22
35mm lens

FIGURE 7.19
Using a tripod combined with a small aperture, I was able to get this 1.3-second exposure and make the water look silky smooth.

SETTING UP FOR A WATERFALL SHOT

1. Attach the camera to your tripod, then compose and focus your shot.
2. For the best quality, make sure the ISO is set to 100.
3. Using Av mode, set your aperture to the smallest opening (such as f/22 or f/36).
4. Press the shutter button halfway so the camera takes a meter reading.
5. Check to see if the shutter speed is 1/15 of a second or slower.
6. Take a photo and then check the image on the LCD.

If the water is blinking on the LCD, indicating a loss of detail in the highlights, then use the Exposure Compensation feature (as discussed earlier in this chapter) to bring details back into the waterfall. You will need to have the Highlight Alert feature turned on to check for overexposure (see "How I Shoot" in Chapter 4).

There is a possibility that you will not be able to have a shutter speed that is long enough to capture a smooth, silky effect, especially if you are shooting in bright daylight conditions. To overcome this obstacle, you need a filter for your lens—either a polarizing filter or a neutral density filter. The polarizing filter redirects wavelengths of light to create more vibrant and accurate colors, reduce reflections, and darken blue skies. It is a handy filter for landscape work. The neutral density filter is typically just a dark piece of glass that serves to darken the scene by one, two, or three stops. This allows you to use slower shutter speeds during bright conditions. Think of it as sunglasses for your camera lens. You will find more discussion on filters in the bonus chapter "Pimp My Ride."

DIRECTING THE VIEWER: A WORD ABOUT COMPOSITION

As a photographer, it's your job to lead the viewer through your image. You accomplish this by utilizing the principles of composition, which is the arrangement of elements in the scene that draws the viewer's eye through your image and holds their attention. As the director of this viewing, you need to understand how people see, and then use that information to focus their attention on the most important elements in your image.

There is a general order in which we look at elements in a photograph. The first is brightness. The eye wants to travel to the brightest object within a scene. So if you have a bright sky, it's probably the first place the eye will travel to. The second order of attention is sharpness. Sharp, detailed elements will get more attention than soft, blurry areas. Finally, the eye will move to vivid colors while leaving the dull, flat colors for last. It is important to know these essentials in order to grab—and keep—the viewer's attention and then direct them through the frame.

In **Figure 7.20**, the eye is drawn to the bright white cloud in the middle of the frame. From there, it is pulled toward the sharpness and color of the large boulder that is anchoring the lower-left portion of the image. The eye moves around the curved section of stone at the bottom of the frame, where it is then lifted back up to the sky and clouds, right back to the beginning. The elements within the image all help to keep the eye moving but never leave the frame.

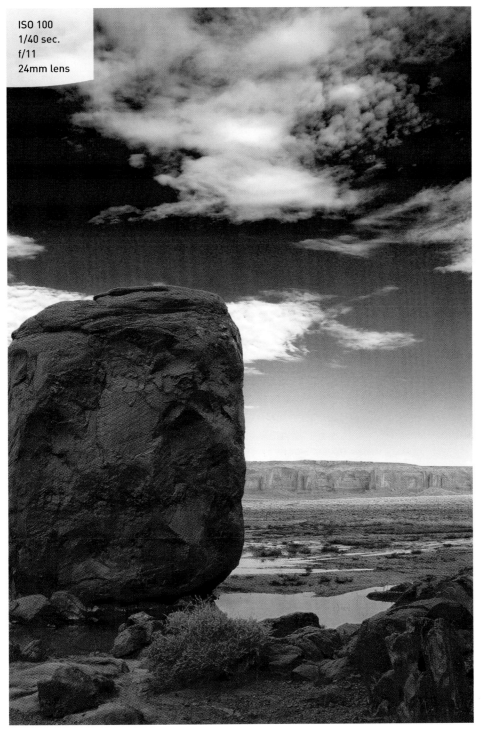

ISO 100
1/40 sec.
f/11
24mm lens

FIGURE 7.20
The composition of the elements pulls the viewer's eyes around the image, leading from one element to the next in a circular pattern.

RULE OF THIRDS

There are, in fact, quite a few philosophies concerning composition. The easiest one to begin with is known as the "rule of thirds." Using this principle, you simply divide your viewfinder into thirds by imagining two horizontal and two vertical lines that divide the frame equally.

The key to using this method of composition is to have your main subject located at or near one of the intersecting points (**Figure 7.21**).

FIGURE 7.21
With the rule-of-thirds grid atop this image, you can see that I composed the shot so that the mountain peak is at the top-left intersection and the shoreline is along the bottom third.

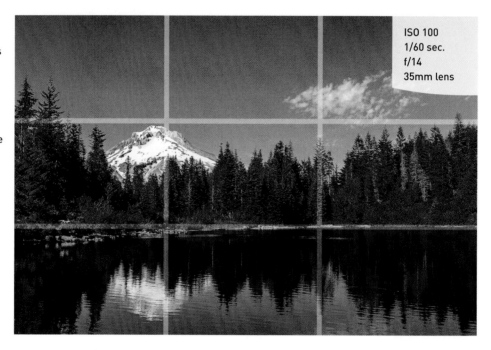

ISO 100
1/60 sec.
f/14
35mm lens

By placing your subject near these intersecting lines, you are giving the viewer space to move within the frame. The one thing you don't want to do is place your subject smack dab in the middle of the frame. This is sometimes referred to as "bull's eye" composition, and it requires the right subject matter for it to work. It's not always wrong, but it will usually be less appealing and may not hold the viewer's focus.

Speaking of the middle of the frame: the other general rule of thirds deals with horizon lines. Generally speaking, you should position the horizon one third of the way up or down in the frame. Splitting the frame in half by placing your horizon in the middle of the picture is akin to placing the subject in the middle of the frame—it doesn't lend a sense of importance to either the sky or the ground.

In **Figure 7.22**, I incorporated the rule of thirds by aligning my horizon in the top third of the frame with the varying landscape textures occupying the bottom two-thirds. In doing so, I have created a sense of depth in the image. By selecting the right lens focal length (14mm, in this instance) and the right vantage point, I was able to place my horizon line so that it gives the greatest emphasis on the subject.

ISO 400
1/125 sec.
f/9
14mm lens

FIGURE 7.22
Placing the horizon of this image in the top third of the frame places emphasis on the landscape below.

CREATING DEPTH

Because a photograph is a flat, two-dimensional space, you need to create a sense of depth by using the elements in the scene to create a three-dimensional feel. This is accomplished by including different and distinct spaces for the eye to travel: a foreground, middle ground, and background. By using these three spaces, you draw the viewer in and render depth to your image.

The hilly scene in northern California shown in **Figure 7.23** illustrates this well. The tree strongly defines the foreground area, the shadowy hills help separate the tree from the middle ground, and the sky gives a great blue background that contrasts with the warm tones of the late afternoon sun.

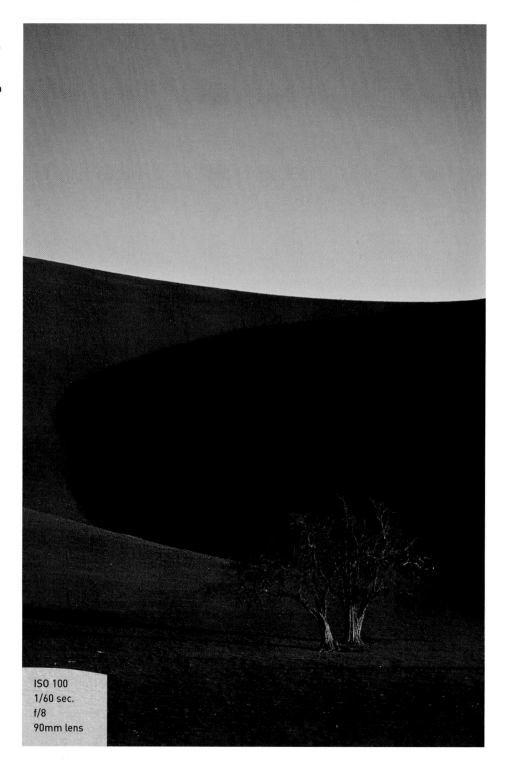

FIGURE 7.23
The tree, shadow, sloping hills, and sky all add to the feeling of depth in the image.

ISO 100
1/60 sec.
f/8
90mm lens

ADVANCED TECHNIQUES TO EXPLORE

This section comes with a warning attached. All of the techniques and topics up to this point have been centered on your camera. The following two sections, covering panoramas and high dynamic range (HDR) images, require you to use image-processing software to complete the photograph. They are, however, important enough that you should know how to correctly shoot for success should you choose to explore these two popular techniques.

SHOOTING PANORAMAS

If you have ever visited the Grand Canyon, you know just how large and wide open it truly is—so much so that it would be difficult to capture its splendor in just one frame. The same can be said for a mountain range or a cityscape or any extremely wide vista. There are two methods that you can use to capture the feeling of this type of scene.

THE "FAKE" PANORAMA

The first method is to shoot as wide as you can and then crop out the top and bottom portion of the frame. Panoramic images are generally two or three times wider than a normal image.

CREATING A FAKE PANORAMA

1. To create the look of a panorama, find your widest lens focal length. If you're using the kit lens that came with the T4i, it would be the 18mm setting on the 18–55mm kit lens.

2. Using the guidelines discussed earlier in the chapter, compose and focus your scene, and select the smallest aperture possible.

3. Shoot your image. That's all there is to it from a photography standpoint.

4. Then, open the image in your favorite image-processing software and crop the extraneous foreground and sky from the image, leaving you with a wide panorama of the scene.

Figure 7.24 shows an example using a photo taken in Death Valley.

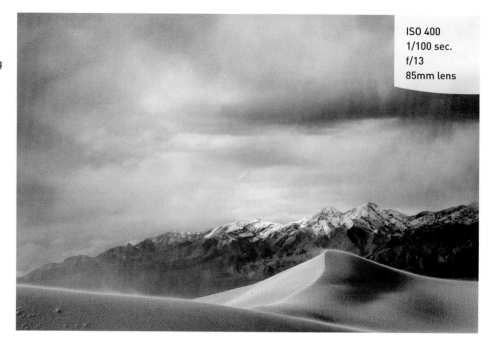

ISO 400
1/100 sec.
f/13
85mm lens

As you can see, the image was shot with a lot of headroom, which includes a large portion of the clouds. It looked like a good crop at the time, but after opening it in my post-processing software I had second thoughts. I opened the Crop tool, took off the top two-thirds of the frame, and came up with a panorama that is much more dynamic and visually interesting (**Figure 7.25**).

FIGURE 7.25
Cropping adds more impact and makes for a more appealing image.

THE MULTIPLE-IMAGE PANORAMA

The reason the previous method is sometimes referred to as a "fake" panorama is because it is made with a standard-size frame and then cropped down to a narrow perspective. To shoot a true panorama, you need to use either a special panorama camera that shoots a very wide frame, or the following method, which requires the combining of multiple frames.

The multiple-image pano has gained in popularity in the past few years; this is principally because of advances in image-processing software. Many software options are available now that will take multiple images, align them, and then "stitch" them into a single panoramic image. The real key to shooting a multiple-image pano is to overlap your shots by about 30 percent from one frame to the next (**Figures 7.26** and **7.27**).

It is possible to handhold the camera while capturing your images, but the best method for capturing great panoramic images is to use a tripod.

Now that you have your series of overlapping images, you can import them into your image-processing software to stitch them together and create a single panoramic image.

SHOOTING PROPERLY FOR A MULTIPLE-IMAGE PANORAMA

1. Mount your camera on your tripod and make sure it is level.

2. Choose a focal length for your lens that is, ideally, somewhere between 35mm and 50mm. (I used an 18mm here, which worked well, but a wide-angle lens can distort the edges of the images, making it harder to stitch them together.)

3. In Av mode, use a very small aperture for the greatest depth of field. Take a meter reading of a bright part of the scene, and make note of it.

4. Now change your camera to Manual mode (M), and dial in the aperture and shutter speed that you obtained in the previous step.

5. Set your lens to manual focus, and then focus your lens for the area of interest using the HFD method of finding a point one-third of the way into the scene. (If you use the autofocus, you risk getting different points of focus from image to image, which will make the image stitching more difficult for the software.) If you want to use the autofocus, just remember to set the lens to MF before shooting your images.

6. While carefully panning your camera, shoot your images to cover the entire area of the scene from one end to the other, leaving a 30 percent overlap from one frame to the next.

FIGURE 7.26
Here you see the makings of a panorama, with four shots overlapping by about 30 percent from frame to frame.

ISO 100
1/50 sec.
f/22
18mm lens

FIGURE 7.27
I used Adobe Photoshop to combine all of the exposures into one large panoramic image.

SHOOTING HIGH DYNAMIC RANGE (HDR) IMAGES

One of the more recent trends in digital photography is the use of high dynamic range (HDR) to capture the full range of tonal values in your final image. Typically, when you photograph a scene that has a wide range of tones from shadows to highlights, you have to make a decision regarding which tonal values you are going to emphasize, and then adjust your exposure accordingly. This is because your camera has a limited dynamic range, at least as compared to the human eye. HDR photography allows you to capture multiple exposures for the highlights, shadows, and midtones and then combine them into a single image using software (**Figures 7.28** through **7.31**). A number of software applications allow you to combine the images and then perform a process called "tonemapping," whereby the complete range of exposures is represented in a single image. I will not be covering the software applications, but I will explore the process of shooting a scene to help you render properly captured images for the HDR process. Note that using a tripod is absolutely necessary for this technique, since you need to have perfect alignment of each image when they are combined.

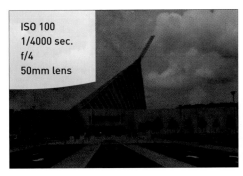

ISO 100
1/4000 sec.
f/4
50mm lens

ISO 100
1/1000 sec.
f/4
50mm lens

FIGURE 7.28
Underexposing two stops will render more detail in the highlight areas of the clouds and sky.

FIGURE 7.29
This is the normal exposure as dictated by the camera meter.

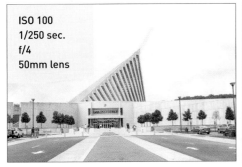

ISO 100
1/250 sec.
f/4
50mm lens

FIGURE 7.30
Overexposing by two stops ensures that the darker areas are exposed to get detail in the shadows.

FIGURE 7.31
This is the final HDR image that was rendered from the three other exposures you see here.

SETTING UP FOR SHOOTING AN HDR IMAGE

1. Set your ISO to 100 if possible to ensure clean, noise-free images.

2. Set your program mode to Av. During the shooting process, you will be taking three shots of the same scene, creating an overexposed image, an underexposed image, and a normal exposure. Since the camera is going to be adjusting the exposure, you want it to make changes to the shutter speed, not the aperture, so that your depth of field is consistent.

3. Set your camera file format to RAW. This is extremely important because the RAW format contains a much larger range of exposure values than a JPEG file, and the HDR software will need this information.

4. Change your shooting mode to Continuous. This will allow you to capture your exposures quickly. Even though you will be using a tripod, there is always a chance that something within your scene will be moving (like clouds or leaves). Shooting in the Continuous mode minimizes any subject movement between frames.

5. Adjust the auto exposure bracket (AEB) mode to shoot three exposures in two-stop increments. To do this, press the Q button and navigate to the Exposure comp./AEB setting (**A**).

6. Press the Set button and then turn the Main dial to the right until the AEB indicators move all the way out to –2 and +2 (**B**). Press the Set button to lock in your changes.

7. Focus the camera using the manual focus method discussed earlier in the chapter, compose your shot, secure the tripod, and hold down the shutter button until the camera has fired three consecutive times.

A

B

A software program—such as Adobe Photoshop, Photomatix Pro, or Nik's HDR Efex Pro—can now process your exposure-bracketed images into a single HDR file. You can find more information on HDR photography and creating HDR images in the Tutorials section at www.photowalkpro.com.

BRACKETING YOUR EXPOSURES

In HDR, *bracketing* is the process of capturing a series of exposures at different stop intervals. You can bracket your exposures even if you aren't going to be using HDR. Sometimes this is helpful when you have a tricky lighting situation and want to ensure that you have just the right exposure to capture the look you're after. You can bracket in increments as small as a third of a stop. This means that you can capture several images with very subtle exposure variances and then decide later which one is best.

Chapter 7 Assignments

We've covered a lot of ground in this chapter, so it's definitely time to put this knowledge to work in order to get familiar with these new camera settings and techniques.

Comparing depth of field: Wide-angle vs. telephoto

You should practice using the hyper focal distance of your lens to maximize the depth of field. You can do this by picking a focal length to work with on your lens. If you have a zoom lens, try using the longest length. Compose your image and find an object to focus on. Set your aperture to f/22 and take a photo.

Now do the same thing with the zoom lens at its widest focal length. Use the same aperture and focus point.

Review the images and compare the depth of field when using a wide-angle focal length as opposed to a telephoto focal length. Try this again with a large aperture as well.

Applying hyper focal distance to your landscapes

Pick a scene that has objects that are near the camera position as well as something that is clearly defined in the background. Try using a wide to medium-wide focal length for this (18–35mm). Use a small aperture and focus on the object in the foreground; then recompose and take a shot. Without moving the camera position, use the object in the background as your point of focus and take another shot. Finally, find a point that is one-third of the way into the frame from near to far and use that as the focus point. Compare all of the images to see which method delivered the greatest range of depth of field.

Using Live View and the rule of thirds

Using the Live View grid, practice shooting while placing your main subject in one of the intersecting line locations. Then take some comparison shots with the same subject in the middle of the frame.

Share your results with the book's Flickr group!

Join the group here: flickr.com/groups/t4i650dfromsnapshotstogreatshots

8

TO THE ARME

ISO 800
1/15 sec.
f/10
35mm lens

Mood Lighting

SHOOTING WHEN THE LIGHTS GET LOW

There is no reason to put your camera away when the sun goes down. Your T4i has some great features that let you work with available light as well as the built-in flash. In this chapter, we will explore ways to push your camera's technology to the limit in order to capture great photos in difficult lighting situations. We will also explore the use of flash and how best to utilize your built-in flash features to improve your photography. But let's first look at working with low-level available light.

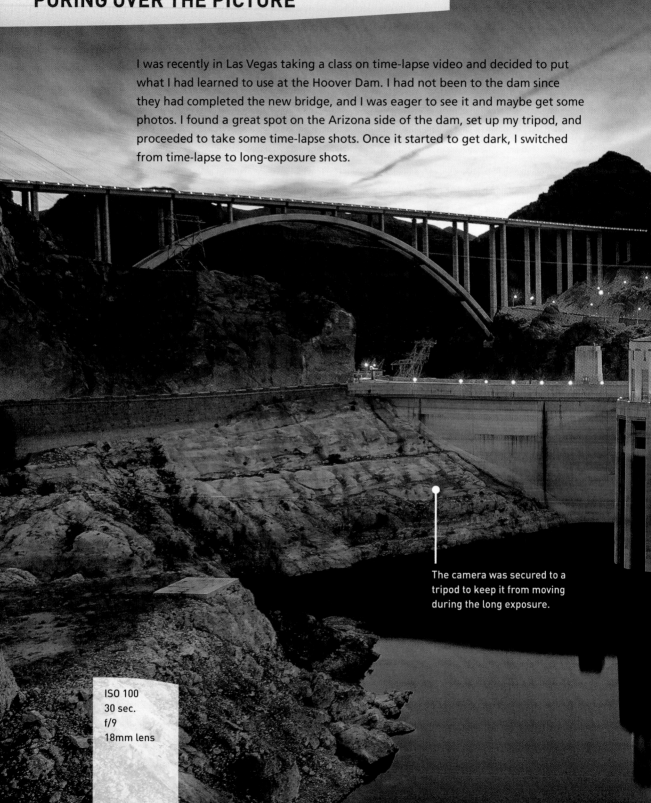

PORING OVER THE PICTURE

I was recently in Las Vegas taking a class on time-lapse video and decided to put what I had learned to use at the Hoover Dam. I had not been to the dam since they had completed the new bridge, and I was eager to see it and maybe get some photos. I found a great spot on the Arizona side of the dam, set up my tripod, and proceeded to take some time-lapse shots. Once it started to get dark, I switched from time-lapse to long-exposure shots.

The camera was secured to a tripod to keep it from moving during the long exposure.

ISO 100
30 sec.
f/9
18mm lens

While I have to admit that I prefer to shoot most of my photos using natural light, there are advantages to using a flash at times. A flash will let you capture images that just aren't possible without one. You can also use a flash to make the light interact with your subject in ways that you could never do using natural light. This shot was taken during the day but with the subject standing in the shade. By using an off-camera flash, I was able to add a soft, beautiful light that wraps around her face while still keeping the background dark.

Using a small aperture made the background dark.

The flash was fired through a diffusion panel to soften the light.

The flash was positioned so there would be a nice catchlight in the eyes.

A telephoto lens was used to get a tight crop of the subject without having to be in her face.

ISO 100
1/60 sec.
f/11
105mm lens

RAISING THE ISO: THE SIMPLE SOLUTION

Let's begin with the obvious way to keep shooting when the lights get low: raising the ISO (**Figure 8.1**). By now you know how to change the ISO: just press the ISO button on the top of the camera and turn the Main dial to adjust. In typical shooting situations, you should keep the ISO in the 100–800 range. This will keep your pictures nice and clean by keeping the digital noise to a minimum. But as the available light gets low, you might find yourself working in the higher ranges of the ISO scale, which could lead to more noise in your image.

FIGURE 8.1
The light inside this Metro stop was fairly dim and forced me to raise the ISO to get the shot without having to use flash.

ISO 1600
1/40 sec.
f/3.2
18mm lens

You could use the flash, but that has a limited range (15–20 feet) that might not work for you. Also, you could be in a situation where flash is prohibited or at least frowned upon, like at a wedding or in a museum.

And what about a tripod in combination with a long shutter speed? That is also an option, and we'll cover it a little further into the chapter. The problem with using a tripod and a slow shutter speed in low-light photography, though, is that it performs best when subjects aren't moving. Besides, try to set up a tripod in a Metro station and see how quickly you grab the attention of the security guards.

So if the only choice to get the shot is to raise the ISO to 800 or higher, make sure that you turn on the High ISO Speed Noise Reduction feature. This menu function is set to

Standard by default, but as you start using higher ISO values you should consider changing it to the Strong setting. (See Chapter 7 for setting the noise-reduction features.)

To see the effect of High ISO Speed Noise Reduction, you need to zoom in and take a closer look (**Figures 8.2** and **8.3**).

Raising the noise reduction to the Strong setting slightly increases the processing time for your images, so if you are shooting in the Continuous drive mode you might see a little reduction in the speed of your frames per second.

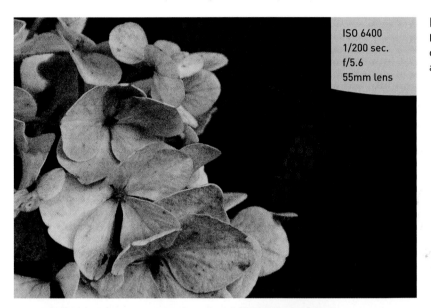

ISO 6400
1/200 sec.
f/5.6
55mm lens

FIGURE 8.2
Here is an enlargement of a flower shot without any ISO noise reduction.

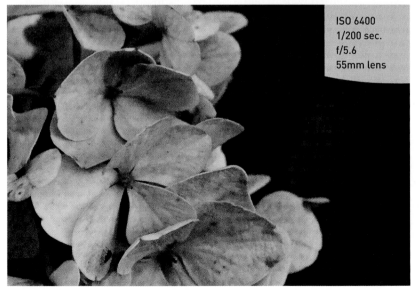

ISO 6400
1/200 sec.
f/5.6
55mm lens

FIGURE 8.3
Here is the same flower with noise reduction set to Strong.

NOISE REDUCTION SAVES SPACE

When shooting at very high ISO settings, running High ISO Speed NR at the Standard or Strong setting can save you space on your memory card. If you are saving your photos as JPEGs, the camera will compress the information in the image to take up less space. When you have excessive noise, you can literally add megabytes to the file size. This is because the camera has to deal with more information: it views the noise in the image as photo information and, therefore, tries not to lose that information during the compression process. That means more noise equals bigger files. So not only will turning on the High ISO Speed NR feature improve the look of your image, it will also save you some space so you can take a few more shots.

USING VERY HIGH ISOS

Is ISO 12800 just not enough for you? Well in that case, you will need to turn on the ISO Expansion setting. This setting opens up another stop of ISO, raising the new limit to an incredible 25600. The highest setting will not appear in your ISO scale as a number, but as H for 25600.

SETTING UP THE ISO EXPANSION FEATURE

1. Press the Menu button and locate the Custom Functions screen (**A**).

2. The ISO Expansion setting is located in the C. Fn I: Exposure section. Highlight it and press Set.

3. Locate the ISO Expansion menu and change the setting from Off to On (**B**).

4. Press the Menu button twice to exit, then press the ISO button to find the additional ISO setting of H (25600).

A word of warning about the expanded ISO settings: although it is great to have high ISO settings available during low-light shooting, they should always be your last resort. Even with the High ISO Speed NR turned on, the amount of visible noise will be extremely high. I can't think of a situation where I ever needed to use the 25600 (H) setting, but you might find yourself at a nighttime sporting event under the lights, which would require an ISO of 3200 or 6400 to improve your shutter speeds and capture the action (**Figure 8.4**).

Manual Callout

For a table listing all of the programmable custom functions, including the ISO Expansion feature, turn to page 293 in your owner's manual.

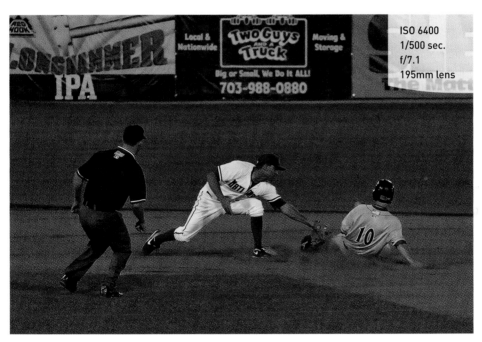

ISO 6400
1/500 sec.
f/7.1
195mm lens

FIGURE 8.4
The only way to get a fast-enough shutter speed during this night-time baseball game was to raise the ISO to 6400.

STABILIZING THE SITUATION

If you purchased your camera with one of the new image stabilization (IS) lenses, you already own a great tool to squeeze two stops of exposure out of your camera when shooting without a tripod (**Figure 8.5**). Typically, the average person can handhold their camera down to about 1/60 of a second before blurriness results due to hand shake. As the length of the lens is increased (or zoomed), the ability to handhold at slow shutter speeds (1/60 and slower) and still get sharp images is further reduced.

FIGURE 8.5
Set the Stabilizer switch to the On position when using longer shutter speeds while handholding your camera.

The Canon IS lenses contain small gyro sensors and servo-actuated optical elements, which correct for camera shake and stabilize the image. The IS function is so good that it is possible to improve your handheld photography by two or three stops, meaning that if you are pretty solid at a shutter speed of 1/60, the IS feature lets you shoot at 1/15 and possibly even 1/8 of a second (**Figures 8.6** and **8.7**).

FIGURE 8.6
This image was shot handheld with the IS turned off.

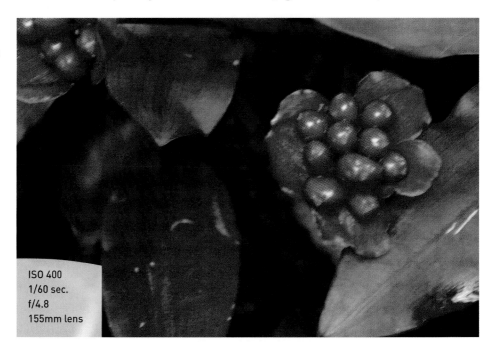

ISO 400
1/60 sec.
f/4.8
155mm lens

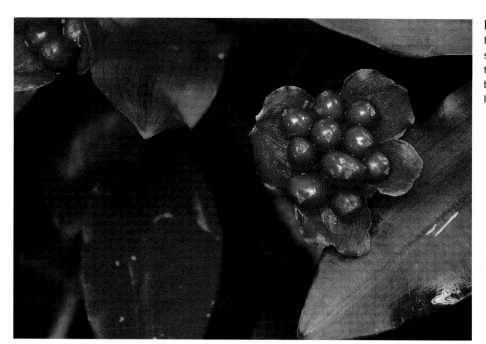

SELF-TIMER

Whether you are shooting with a tripod or even resting your camera on a wall, you can increase the sharpness of your pictures by taking your hands out of the equation. Whenever you use your finger to depress the shutter release button, you are increasing the chance that there will be a little bit of shake in your image. To eliminate this possibility, try setting your camera up to use the self-timer. To turn on the self-timer, press the Q button to activate the Quick Control screen, highlight the drive mode icon, and then turn the Main dial until the self-timer icon appears. There are three self-timer modes to choose from. I generally use the 2-second mode to cut down on time between exposures.

FIGURE 8.8
Focusing on the night sky is best done in manual focus mode.

ISO 200
30 sec.
f/5.6
18mm lens

FOCUSING IN LOW LIGHT

The T4i has a great focusing system, but occasionally the light levels might be too low for the camera to achieve an accurate focus. There are a few things that you can do to overcome this obstacle.

First, you should know that the camera utilizes contrast in the viewfinder to establish a point of focus. This is why your camera will not be able to focus when you point it at a white wall or a cloudless sky; it simply can't find any contrast in the scene to work with. Knowing this, you might be able to use a single focus point in One Shot mode to find an area of contrast that is at the same distance as your subject. You can then hold that focus by holding down the shutter button halfway and recomposing your image.

Then there are those times when there just isn't anything there for you to focus on. A perfect example of this would be a fireworks display. If you point your lens to the night sky in any automatic focus (AF) mode, it will just keep searching for—and not finding—a focus point. On these occasions, you can simply turn off the autofocus feature and manually focus the lens (**Figure 8.8**). Look for the AF/MF switch on the side of the lens and slide it to the MF position.

Don't forget to put it back in AF mode at the end of your shoot.

FOCUS ASSIST

Another way to ensure good focus is to enable the T4i's Focus Assist mode. Focus Assist uses a short burst from your pop-up flash to shine some light on the scene, which assists the autofocus system in locating more detail. This feature is automatically activated when shooting in the Basic zone (except in Landscape, Sports, and Flash Off modes for the following reasons: in Landscape mode, the subject is usually too far away; in Sports mode, the subject is probably moving; and in Flash Off mode, you've disabled the flash entirely). Focus Assist should be enabled by default, but you can check the menu just to make sure.

TURNING ON THE FOCUS ASSIST FEATURE

1. Press the Menu button, use the Main dial to get to the Custom Functions menu tab, highlight Custom Functions, and press the Set button (**A**).

A

2. Use the left/right Cross keys to get to the C. Fn III: Autofocus/Drive AF-assist beam firing feature and see the current setting for this function (**B**).

3. If it is not enabled, press the Set button, highlight Enable, and press the Set button again.

4. To use it when working in the Creative zone, simply press the flash button to raise the pop-up flash.

5. With the flash in the "up" position, press the shutter button to focus; Focus Assist will activate if necessary.

If you don't want the flash to fire during the actual exposure, you must first disable the flash.

DISABLING THE FLASH

1. Press the Menu button and then scroll the Main dial to highlight the first shooting menu (far left).

2. Scroll down to Flash control, and press the Set button (**A**).

3. Select Flash firing, and press the Set button (**B**).

4. Set the Flash firing option to Disable (**C**).

SHOOTING LONG EXPOSURES

We have covered some of the techniques for shooting in low light, so let's go through the process of capturing a night or low-light scene for maximum image quality (**Figure 8.9**). The first thing to consider is that in order to shoot in low light with a low ISO, you will need to use shutter speeds that are longer than you could possibly handhold (longer than 1/15 of a second). This will require the use of a tripod or stable surface for you to place your camera on. For maximum quality, the ISO should be low—somewhere at or below 400. The long exposure noise reduction should be turned on to minimize the effects of exposing for longer durations. (To set this up, see Chapter 7.)

Once you have the noise reduction turned on, set your camera to Aperture Priority (Av) mode. That way, you can concentrate on the aperture that you believe is most appropriate and let the camera determine the best shutter speed. If it is too dark for the autofocus to function properly, try manually focusing. Finally, consider using a cable release (see the bonus chapter "Pimp My Ride") to activate the shutter. If you don't have one, check out the sidebar on using the self-timer (page 213). Once you shoot the image, you may notice some lag time before it is displayed on the rear LCD. This is due to the noise-reduction process, which can take anywhere from a fraction of a second up to 30 seconds, depending on the length of the exposure.

ISO 100
30 sec.
f/9
18mm lens

FIGURE 8.9
A long exposure and a tripod were necessary to capture this twilight photo of the Hoover Dam.

The basic idea behind the term *flash synchronization* (*flash sync* for short) is that when you take a photograph using the flash, the camera needs to ensure that the shutter is fully open at the time that the flash goes off. This is not an issue if you are using a long shutter speed such as 1/15 of a second but does become more critical for fast shutter speeds. To ensure that the flash and shutter are synchronized so that the flash is going off while the shutter is open, the T4i implements a top sync speed of 1/200 of a second. This means that when you are using the flash, you will not be able to have your shutter speed set any faster than 1/200. If you did use a faster shutter speed, the shutter would actually start closing before the flash fired, which would cause a black, underexposed area to appear in the frame where the light from the flash was blocked.

USING THE BUILT-IN FLASH

There are going to be times when you have to turn to your camera's built-in flash to get the shot. The pop-up flash on the T4i is not extremely powerful, but with the camera's advanced metering system it does a pretty good job of lighting up the night...or just filling in the shadows.

If you are working in the Creative zone, you will have to turn the flash on for yourself. To do this, just press the pop-up flash button located on the front of the camera (**Figure 8.10**). Once the flash is up, it is ready to go (**Figure 8.11**). It's that simple.

FIGURE 8.10
A quick press of the pop-up flash button will release the built-in flash to its ready position.

FIGURE 8.11
The pop-up flash in its ready position.

SHUTTER SPEEDS

The standard flash synchronization speed for your camera is between 1/60 and 1/200 of a second. When you are working with the built-in flash in the Basic zone, the camera will typically use a shutter speed of 1/60 of a second. The exception to this is when you use the Night Portrait mode, which will fire the flash with a slower shutter speed so that some of the ambient light has time to record in the image.

The real key to using the flash to get great pictures is to control the shutter speed. The goal is to balance the light from the flash with the existing light so that everything in the picture has an even illumination. Let's take a look at the shutter speeds for the modes in the Creative zone.

 Program (P): The shutter speed stays at 1/60 of a second. You can make changes to the aperture by pressing the Av button on the back of the camera while turning the Main dial, but you risk over- or underexposing your image.

 Shutter Priority (Tv): You can adjust the shutter speed from as fast as 1/200 of a second all the way down to 30 seconds. The lens aperture will adjust accordingly, but at long exposures the lens will typically be set to its largest aperture.

 Aperture Priority (Av): This mode has three custom settings for adjusting the shutter speed when using the flash, depending on your needs. The whole point of this setting is to allow you to use the aperture of your choice while still getting good flash exposures.

The default value is Auto, which adjusts from 1/200 of a second all the way down to 30 seconds, depending on the available light. As the aperture gets smaller, the shutter speeds will get longer. There are also two speed-limiting settings to choose from. The first is "1/200–1/60 sec. auto." This limits the shutter speed to a maximum duration of 1/60 of a second. If you have the aperture set to an f-stop that has a very small opening for a proper exposure, the shutter speed indicator will flash, letting you know that you are risking underexposure. For all other exposures, the camera will moderate the shutter speed to a selection that is within the 1/60–1/200 range. The other setting is "1/200 sec. (fixed)." This setting maintains a shutter speed of 1/200 of a second no matter what the f-stop is set to. Your flash will try to vary its power output to meet the needs of the setting that you have selected.

SETTING THE SYNC SPEED WHEN USING FLASH IN AV MODE

1. Press the Menu button and go to the first shooting menu. Highlight Flash control, and then press the Set button (**A**).

2. Use the Cross keys to select Flash sync. speed in Av mode, and press the Set button (**B**).

3. Select the Av sync speed that you desire using the Cross keys, and press Set once more (**C**).

A

B

C

Manual (M): Manual mode works the same as Tv mode, with a range of 1/200 of a second down to 30 seconds. The difference, of course, is that you must manually set the f-stop.

METERING MODES

The built-in flash uses a technology called E-TTL II (Evaluative Through The Lens) metering to determine the appropriate amount of flash power to output for a good exposure. When you depress the shutter button, the camera quickly adjusts focus while gathering information from the entire scene to measure the amount of ambient light. As you press the shutter button down completely, a pre-flash occurs to meter the light off the subject from the flash, and a determination is made as to how much power is needed to balance the subject with the ambient light. This applies to all of the modes in the Creative zone, with the exception of Manual mode.

The default setting for the flash meter mode is Evaluative. The meter can also be set to Average mode, but that should probably be avoided. Your best results will come from the E-TTL mode.

But if you have special metering needs, such as a background that is very light or dark, you might consider using the Flash Exposure (FE) Lock to meter off your subject and then recompose your image in the viewfinder.

This feature works much like the Automatic Exposure (AE) Lock function that was discussed in Chapter 6.

FLASH RANGE

Because the pop-up flash is fairly small, it does not have enough power to illuminate a large space (**Figure 8.12**). The effective distance varies depending on the ISO setting. At ISO 100, the range is about 12 feet. This range can be extended to as far as 138 feet when the camera is set to an ISO of 12800. For the best image quality, your ISO setting should not go above 800. Anything higher will begin to introduce excessive noise into your photos.

ISO 400
1/13 sec.
f/3.5
18mm lens

FIGURE 8.12
The pop-up flash was used to fill in the shadows on the elephant, while the long exposure time allowed the ambient light to illuminate the rest of the scene.

USING THE FE LOCK FEATURE

1. Point the camera at the area that you want to base the flash exposure on. This is normally your subject.

2. Press the AE/FE Lock button (✱) (near the top right on the back of the camera) to obtain the exposure setting. The flash will fire a small burst to evaluate the exposure, and you will see "FEL" (Flash Exposure Lock) appear briefly in the viewfinder. The AE/FE Lock symbol (✱) will also appear in the viewfinder next to the flash symbol.

3. Recompose the scene as you like, and press the shutter button completely.

The FE Lock will cancel after each exposure, so you have to repeat these steps each time you need to lock the flash exposure.

Using the Average metering mode might also require that you tweak the flash output by using Flash Exposure Compensation. This is because the camera will be metering the entire scene to set the exposure, so you might have to add or subtract flash power to balance out the scene.

COMPENSATING FOR THE FLASH EXPOSURE

The E-TTL system will usually do an excellent job of balancing the flash and ambient light for your exposure, but it does have the limitation of not knowing what effect you want in your image. You may want more or less flash in a particular shot. You can achieve this by using the Flash Exposure Compensation feature.

Just as with exposure compensation, flash compensation allows you to dial in a change in the flash output in increments of 1/3 of a stop. You will probably use this most often to tone down the effects of your flash, especially when you are using the flash as a subtle fill light (**Figures 8.13** and **8.14**).

ISO 400
1/60 sec.
f/4
200mm lens

ISO 400
1/60 sec.
f/4
200mm lens

FIGURE 8.13
This shot was taken with the pop-up flash set to normal power. As you can see, it was trying too hard to illuminate my subject.

FIGURE 8.14
This image was made with the same camera settings. The difference is that the flash compensation was set to –1.3 stops.

USING THE FLASH EXPOSURE COMPENSATION FEATURE TO CHANGE THE FLASH OUTPUT

1. Press the Q button to activate the Quick Control screen on the LCD.

2. Use the Cross keys to move the cursor to the Flash Exposure Compensation icon.

3. Rotate the Main dial to adjust the flash compensation in 1/3-stop increments (left to subtract and right to add).

4. Press the shutter button halfway to return to shooting mode, and then take the picture.

5. Review your image to see if more or less flash compensation is required, and repeat these steps as necessary.

The Flash Exposure Compensation feature does not reset itself when the camera is turned off, so whatever compensation you have set will remain in effect until you change it. Your only clue that the flash output is changed will be the presence of the Flash Exposure Compensation symbol on the rear LCD, so make sure you check it. It will disappear when there is zero compensation set.

REDUCING RED-EYE

We've all seen the result of using on-camera flashes when shooting people: the dreaded red-eye! This demonic effect is the result of the light from the flash entering the pupil and then reflecting back as an eerie red glow. The closer the flash is to the lens, the greater the chance that you will get red-eye. This is especially true when it is dark and the subject's pupils are dilated. There are two ways to combat this problem. The first is to get the flash away from the lens. That's not really an option, though, if you are using the pop-up flash. Therefore, you will need to turn to the Red-Eye Reduction feature.

This is a simple feature that shines a light from the camera at the subject, causing their pupils to shrink, thus eliminating or reducing the effects of red-eye (**Figure 8.15**).

The feature is set to Off by default and needs to be turned on in the shooting menu.

TURN ON THE LIGHTS!

When shooting indoors, another way to reduce red-eye, or just shorten the length of time that the reduction lamp needs to be shining into your subject's eyes, is to turn on a lot of lights. The brighter the ambient light levels, the smaller the subject's pupils will be. This will reduce the time necessary for the red-eye reduction lamp to shine. It will also allow you to take more candid pictures because your subjects won't be required to stare at the red-eye lamp while waiting for their pupils to reduce.

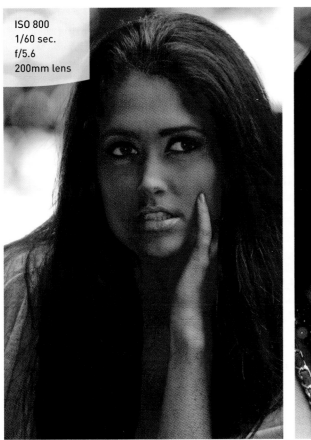

ISO 800
1/60 sec.
f/5.6
200mm lens

FIGURE 8.15

The picture on the left did not utilize Red-Eye Reduction, thus the glowing red eyes. Notice that the pupils in the image on the right, without red-eye, are smaller as a result of using the red-eye reduction lamp.

TURNING ON THE RED-EYE REDUCTION FEATURE

1. Press the Menu button and then turn the Main dial to get to the first shooting menu.

2. Use the Cross keys to scroll down to the Red-eye reduc. setting (**A**).

A

3. Press the Set button, use the Cross keys to select Enable, and press the Set button again (**B**).

4. Press the Menu button twice, or the shutter release button, to return to shooting mode.

To get the full benefit of the Red-Eye Reduction feature, you should hold down the shutter button halfway, which causes the reduction light to shine into your subject's eyes. A small scale will appear in the viewfinder, showing how long to hold the shutter button before pressing completely. Once the countdown scale has reduced down to nothing, press the shutter button completely to take the picture.

Truth be told, I rarely shoot with Red-Eye Reduction turned on because of the time it takes before being able to take a picture. If I am after candid shots and have to use the flash, I will take my chances on red-eye and try to fix the problem in my image-processing software. The Canon Image Browser software that comes with your T4i has a red-eye reduction feature that works really well.

2ND CURTAIN SYNC

There are two flash synchronization modes in the T4i: 1st Curtain and 2nd Curtain. You may be asking, "What in the world does synchronization do, and what are these 'curtains'?" Good question.

When your camera fires, there are two curtains that open and close to make up the shutter. The first curtain moves out of the way, exposing the camera sensor to the light. At the end of the exposure, the second curtain moves in front of the sensor, ending that picture cycle. In flash photography, timing is extremely important because the flash fires in milliseconds and the shutter is usually opening in tenths or hundredths of a second. To make sure these two functions happen in order, the camera usually fires the flash just as the first curtain moves out of the way (see the sidebar "Flash Sync" earlier in this chapter).

In 2nd Curtain Sync mode, the flash will not fire until just before the second shutter curtain ends the exposure. So, why have this mode at all? Well, there might be times when you want to have a longer exposure to balance out the light from the background to go with the subject needing the flash. Imagine taking a photograph of a friend standing in Times Square at night with all the traffic moving about and the bright lights of the buildings and signs overhead. If the flash fires at the beginning of the exposure and then the objects around the subject move, those objects will often blur the subject a bit. If the camera is set to 2nd Curtain Sync, though, all of the movement of the existing light is recorded first, and then the subject is "frozen" by the flash at the end by the exposure.

There is no right or wrong to it. It's just a decision on what type of effect you would like to create. Many times, 2nd Curtain Sync is used for artistic purposes or to record movement in the scene without it overlapping the flash-exposed subject (**Figure 8.16**). To make sure that the main subject is always getting the final pop of the flash, I leave my camera set to 2nd Curtain Sync.

ISO 400
1/10 sec.
f/4
18mm lens

FIGURE 8.16
The effect of using 2nd Curtain Sync is most evident during long flash exposures.

Using 1st Curtain Sync mode will give a similar effect, but the flash will fire at the beginning of the sequence (**Figure 8.17**). If you do intend to use a long exposure with 1st Curtain synchronization, you need to have your subject remain fairly still so that any movement that occurs after the flash goes off will be minimized in the image.

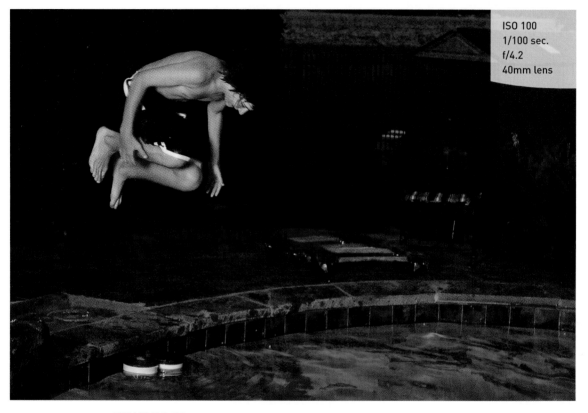

ISO 100
1/100 sec.
f/4.2
40mm lens

FIGURE 8.17
1st Curtain Sync is the default setting for flash photography and can be used for most of your flash photography needs.

SETTING YOUR FLASH SYNC MODE

1. Press the Menu button, navigate to the first shooting menu, select Flash control, and press Set (**A**).

2. Use the Cross keys to select the Built-in flash func. setting, and then press the Set button (**B**).

3. Use the Cross keys once again to select the Shutter sync option (**C**), and then select either the 1st or 2nd Curtain option for the type of flash sync that you desire (**D**).

USING AN EXTERNAL SPEEDLITE

One of the more exciting features of the T4i is its ability to control an off-camera flash by using the pop-up flash as the wireless controller. In years past, you needed to mount a controller flash unit (such as the ST-E2 transmitter) on top of the camera, which meant spending additional money. Now you can simply purchase one of the wireless-enabled Speedlites, like the 320EX, and have complete control to move it away from the camera.

The biggest benefit to doing this is that you can get more natural-looking light by having the flash moved to the side of the camera. This gives you better and more natural shadows. You can also do things like fire the external flash through umbrellas, softboxes, or simple diffusion panels to make the quality of light much softer and more complimentary to your subject (**Figure 8.18**).

FIGURE 8.18
By moving the flash away from the camera and firing it through a diffusion panel, you can achieve a quality of light that is much more flattering to your subjects.

ISO 100
1/60 sec.
f/11
105mm lens

USING OFF-CAMERA FLASH

In order to use an off-camera Speedlite, you need to do two things. First, purchase the Speedlite. There are several models that allow you to use the wireless feature, and they range in price from around $225 for the 320EX all the way up to $600 for the top-of-the-line model, the 600EX-RT. Personally, I am a fan of the 320EX (**Figure 8.19**) because it has the added benefit of having a built-in LED light that can be used as both a focus-assist lamp and a video-recording light. It also has a pivoting head that allows the light to be bounced off the ceiling to create softer, more flattering light.

FIGURE 8.19
The 320EX is a great Speedlite for starting out with flash.

SETTING UP OFF-CAMERA FLASH

1. Press the Menu button and then select the Flash control option in the first shooting menu (**A**).

2. Using the Cross keys, select the Built-in flash settings option, and press Set (**B**).

3. Select Built-in flash and press Set (**C**).

4. Choose which wireless option you want to use, Easy or Custom (**D**).

5. If you select Easy, set the channel number of the slave unit that you want to control (**E**), and you are ready to start shooting. Simply pop up the built-in flash, turn on the Speedlite and set it to wireless mode, and start shooting. If you want to have more control, choose the Custom setting and adjust as follows.

CUSTOM WIRELESS SETTINGS

1. To gain more control over your wireless slave flash, follow steps 1–4 in the previous section, but select the CustWireless option (**A**).

2. Next, select how you want the built-in flash to operate. If you only want the built-in flash to control the slave unit and not have any effect on the actual image—that is, you don't want the built-in flash to fire—then highlight Wireless func. and press Set (**B**).

3. Select the External speedlite only icon (**C**).

4. Select the channel for the slave unit by highlighting the Channel option, pressing Set, and then using the up/down Cross keys to select the channel of your choice, 1–4 (**D**).

5. Make sure the built-in flash is in the raised position, set up the wireless slave flash by turning it on and setting it to wireless with the appropriate channel, point the slave's wireless sensor at the camera, and start shooting.

Manual Callout

Wireless flash photography is a lot of fun and really lets you expand on the creative possibilities of your photography. You may find that you wish to add additional wireless flashes to your system, which is easily handled with the wireless technology built into your camera. If you want further direction and creative options, check out the Wireless Flash section of your manual (pages 189–199).

FLASH AND GLASS

If you find yourself in a situation where you want to use your flash to shoot through a window or display case, try placing your lens right against the glass so that the reflection of the flash won't be visible in your image (**Figures 8.20** and **8.21**). This is extremely useful in museums and aquariums.

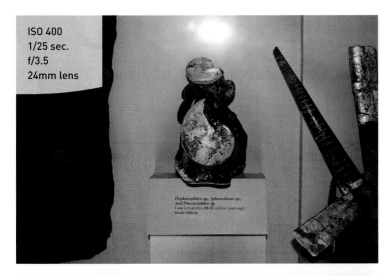

ISO 400
1/25 sec.
f/3.5
24mm lens

FIGURE 8.20
The bright spot at the top of the frame is a result of the flash reflecting off the display case.

ISO 400
1/25 sec.
f/3.5
18mm lens

FIGURE 8.21
To eliminate the reflection, place the lens against the glass or as close to it as possible. This might also require zooming the lens out a little.

Chapter 8 Assignments

Now that we have looked at the possibilities of shooting after dark, it's time to put it all to the test. These assignments cover the full range of shooting possibilities, both with flash and without. Let's get started.

How steady are your hands?

It's important to know just what your limits are in terms of handholding your camera and still getting sharp pictures. This will change depending on the focal length of the lens you are working with. Wider-angle lenses are more forgiving than telephoto lenses, so check this out for your longest and shortest lenses. Using an 18–200mm zoom as an example, set your lens to 200mm and then, with the camera set to ISO 100 and the mode set to Tv, start taking pictures with lower and lower shutter speeds. Review each image on the LCD at a zoomed-in magnification to take note of when you start seeing visible camera shake in your images. It will probably be around 1/125 of a second for a 200mm lens.

Now do the same for the wide-angle setting on the lens. My limit is about 1/30 of a second. These shutter speeds are with the image stabilization feature turned off. If you have an IS lens, try it with and without the IS feature enabled to see just how slow you can set your shutter while getting sharp results.

Pushing your ISO to the extreme

Turn on the ISO Expansion feature. Now find a place to shoot where the ambient light level is low. This could be at night or indoors in a darkened room. Using the mode of your choice, start increasing the ISO from 100 until you get to 25600. Make sure you evaluate the level of noise in your image, especially in the shadow areas. Only you can decide how much noise is acceptable in your pictures. I can tell you from personal experience that I never like to stray above the ISO 800 mark.

Getting rid of the noise

Turn on the High ISO Speed Noise Reduction and repeat the previous assignment. Find your acceptable limits with the noise reduction turned on. Also pay attention to how much detail is lost in your shadows with this function enabled.

Long exposures in the dark

If you don't have a tripod, find a stable place to set your camera outside and try some long exposures. Set your camera to Av mode and then use the self-timer to activate the camera (this will keep you from shaking the camera while pressing the shutter button).

Shoot in an area that has some level of ambient light, be it a streetlight, traffic lights, or even a full moon. The idea is to get some late-night, low-light exposures.

Reducing the noise in your long exposures

Now repeat the last assignment with the Long Exposure Noise Reduction set to On. Now look at the difference in the images that were taken before and after the noise reduction was enabled. For best results, perform this assignment and the previous assignment in the same shooting session using the same subject.

Testing the limits of the pop-up flash

Wait for the lights to get low and then press that pop-up flash button to start using the built-in flash. Try using the different shooting modes to see how they affect your exposures. Use the Flash Exposure Compensation feature to take a series of pictures while adjusting from –2 stops all the way to +2 stops so that you become familiar with how much latitude you will get from this feature.

Getting the red out

Find a friend with some patience and a tolerance for bright lights. Have them sit in a darkened room or outside at night and then take their picture with the flash. Now turn on the Red-Eye Reduction to see if you get better results. Don't forget to wait for the red-eye timer to completely extinguish before taking the picture.

Getting creative with 2nd Curtain Sync

Now it's time for a little creative fun. Set your camera up for 2nd Curtain Sync and start shooting. Moving targets are best. Experiment with Tv and Av modes to lower the shutter speeds and exaggerate the effect. Try using a low ISO so the camera is forced to use longer shutter speeds. Be creative and have some fun!

Share your results with the book's Flickr group!

Join the group here: flickr.com/groups/t4i650dfromsnapshotstogreatshots

9

ISO 400
1/1000 sec.
f/3.8
24mm lens

Creative Compositions

IMPROVE YOUR PICTURES WITH SOUND COMPOSITIONAL ELEMENTS

Creating a great photograph takes more than just using the right settings on your camera. To take your photography to the next level, you need to gain an understanding of how the elements within the frame come together to create a compositionally pleasing image. Composition is the culmination of light, shape, and, to borrow a word from the iconic photographer Jay Maisel, gesture. Composition is a way for you to pull your viewing audience into your image and guide them through the scene. Let's examine some common compositional elements you can use to add interest to your photos.

PORING OVER THE PICTURE

The large aperture setting lets the sharpness fall off to the left area of the frame.

The Cloudy white balance setting warmed up the image.

Getting a good photograph isn't always about the camera settings. It's also about how we frame the image in the viewfinder. When you are out taking photos, it's easy to get lazy and only look at things from eye level, but in doing so you can miss out on new perspectives. This image, taken in the Presidio in San Francisco, was the result of putting my camera down low. Doing so allowed me to capture the beauty of the moss growing on the steps. Getting down at step level gave a much better view and perspective of the scene than I could have captured from a standing position.

I framed the scene so that I would get strong, angular lines from the steps.

The camera was placed low in the frame to emphasize the steps.

ISO 200
1/90 sec.
f/5
24mm lens

PORING OVER THE PICTURE

In landscape photography you can control a lot of things, but when it comes to the weather, you are pretty much stuck. Sometimes you have to just make the most of what you have and look for opportunities to get your shot. This visit to Grand Canyon West was one of those days. After driving for two hours to get there, I was met with wind, clouds, and rain. Luckily, the clouds parted a little and let some sun into the area long enough for me to grab a few quick frames before it started raining again.

I framed the scene with the agave plant in front to add interest to the foreground.

The horizon was placed near the top of the frame to emphasize the canyon and foreground.

The Cloudy white balance setting added warmth to the vegetation.

I used a tripod to stabilize my camera in the strong winds.

ISO 100
1/20 sec.
f/13
18mm lens

DEPTH OF FIELD

Long focal lengths and large apertures allow you to isolate your subject from the chaos that surrounds it. I utilize the Av mode for the majority of my shooting. I also like to use a longer focal length lens to shrink the depth of field to a very narrow area (**Figure 9.1**).

FIGURE 9.1
A large aperture setting can create a shallow depth of field to isolate the subject.

ISO 800
1/125 sec.
f/1.4
50mm lens

The blurred background and foreground force the viewer's eye toward the sharper, in-focus areas, which gives greater emphasis to the subject.

Occasionally, a greater depth of field is required to maintain sharp focus across a greater distance. This might be due to the sheer depth of your subject, where you have objects that are near the camera but sharpness is desired at a greater distance as well (**Figure 9.2**).

Or perhaps you are photographing a reflection in a puddle. With a narrow depth of field, you would only be able to get either the reflected object or the puddle in focus. By making the aperture smaller, you will be able to maintain acceptable sharpness in both areas (**Figure 9.3**).

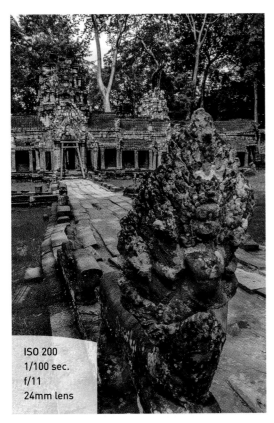

ISO 200
1/100 sec.
f/11
24mm lens

FIGURE 9.2

Getting sharp focus from near to far requires a small aperture setting. A wide-angle lens doesn't hurt either.

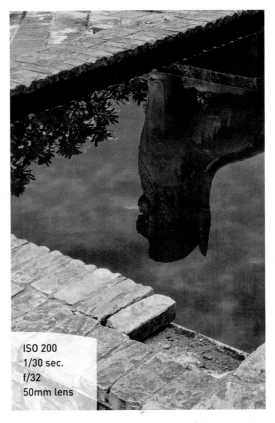

ISO 200
1/30 sec.
f/32
50mm lens

FIGURE 9.3

Getting a distant subject in focus in a reflection, along with the reflective surface, requires a small aperture.

PHOTOGRAPHING REFLECTIONS

A mirror is a two-dimensional surface, so why do I have to focus at a different distance for the image in the mirror? This was one of those questions that drove me crazy when I began to learn about photography. The answer is pretty simple, and it has to do with light. When you focus your lens, you are focusing the light being reflected off a surface onto your camera sensor. So if you wanted to focus on the mirror itself, it would be at one distance, but if you wanted to focus on the subject being reflected, you would have to take into account the distance that the object is from the mirror and then to you. Remember that the light from the subject has to travel all the way to the mirror and then to your lens. This is why a smaller aperture can be required when shooting reflected subjects. Sit in your car and take a few shots of objects in the side view mirrors to see what I mean.

ANGLES

Having strong angular lines in your image can add to the composition, especially when they are juxtaposed to each other (**Figure 9.4**). This can create a tension that is different from the standard horizontal and vertical lines that we are so accustomed to seeing in photos.

FIGURE 9.4
The strong angular lines of the building and shadows create a dynamic composition.

ISO 200
1/100 sec.
f/11
24mm lens

POINT OF VIEW

Sometimes the easiest way to influence your photographs is to simply change your perspective. Instead of always shooting from a standing position, try moving your camera to a place where you normally would not see your subject. Try getting down on your knees or even lying on the ground. This low angle can completely change how you view your subject and can create a new interest in common subjects (**Figure 9.5**).

PATTERNS

Rhythm and balance can be added to your images by finding the patterns in everyday life and concentrating on the elements that rely on geometric influences. Try to find the balance and patterns that often go unnoticed (**Figure 9.6**).

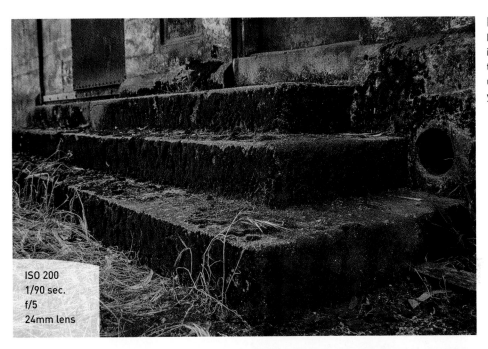

FIGURE 9.5
Put your camera into a position that presents an unfamiliar view of your subject.

ISO 200
1/90 sec.
f/5
24mm lens

ISO 1600
1/20 sec.
f/6.3
18mm lens

FIGURE 9.6
I positioned myself so that I could break up the pattern of the columns with the monument in the background.

COLOR

Color works well as a tool for composition when you have very saturated colors to work with. Some of the best colors are those within the primary palette. Reds, greens, and blues, along with their complementary colors (cyan, magenta, and yellow), can all be used to create visual tension (**Figure 9.7**). This tension between bright colors will add visual excitement, drama, and complexity to your images when combined with other compositional elements.

You can also use a color as a theme for your photography. One of the shots that I am known for is something that I call "the blue sky shot." If I am out shooting when the skies are blue, I can almost guarantee that I will try to use the sky as part of a background for some element of my image (**Figure 9.8**). The blue sky can act as a pleasing color contrast, giving visual interest and isolation to my subject.

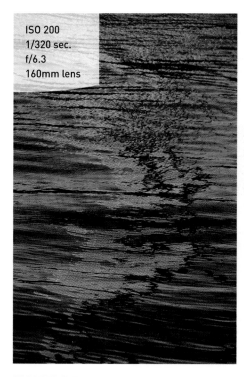

ISO 200
1/320 sec.
f/6.3
160mm lens

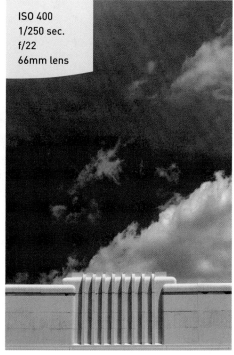

ISO 400
1/250 sec.
f/22
66mm lens

FIGURE 9.7
I loved how the sunbathed reflection of the Washington Monument created a wonderful contrast to the reflection of the blue sky in the water. Combined, they make for a great abstract shot.

FIGURE 9.8
The predominance of the blue sky is used as a balance to the strong art deco design below.

CONTRAST

We just saw that you can use color as a strong compositional tool. One of the most effective uses of color is to combine two contrasting colors that make the eye move back and forth across the image (**Figure 9.9**). There is no exact combination that will work best, but consider using dark and light colors, like red and yellow or blue and yellow, to provide the strongest contrasts.

ISO 400
1/100 sec.
f/5.6
145mm lens

FIGURE 9.9
The slate blue of the roof adds a nice color contrast to the bright orange of the fall foliage.

You can also introduce contrast through different geometric shapes that battle (in a good way) for the attention of the viewer. You can combine circles and triangles, ovals and rectangles, curvy and straight, hard and soft, dark and light, and so many more (**Figure 9.10**). You aren't limited to just one contrasting element either. Combining more than one element of contrast will add even more interest. Look for these contrasting combinations whenever you are out shooting, and then use them to shake up your compositions.

FIGURE 9.10
I loved the contrast of colors in this image combined with the geometric shapes of the kayaks.

ISO 800
1/1000 sec.
f/2.8
155mm lens

LEADING LINES

One way to pull a viewer into your image is to incorporate leading lines. These are elements that come from the edge of the frame and then lead into the image toward the main subject (**Figure 9.11**). This can be the result of vanishing perspective lines, an element such as a river, or some other feature used to move from the outer edge in to the heart of the image.

ISO 400
1/640 sec.
f/5.6
200mm lens

FIGURE 9.11
The lines created by the frame of the boat and the oar lead the eye back to the woman.

SPLITTING THE FRAME

Generally speaking, splitting the frame right down the middle is not necessarily your best option. While it may seem more balanced, it can actually be pretty boring. You should utilize the rule of thirds when deciding how to divide your frame (**Figure 9.12**).

With horizons, a low horizon will give a sense of stability to the image. Typically, this is done when the sky is more appealing than the landscape below (**Figure 9.13**). When the emphasis is to be placed on the landscape, the horizon line should be moved upward in the frame, leaving the bottom two-thirds to the subject.

FIGURE 9.12
The frame is divided equally into thirds, with the agave plants, the canyon ridge line, and the sky positioned along each third of the image.

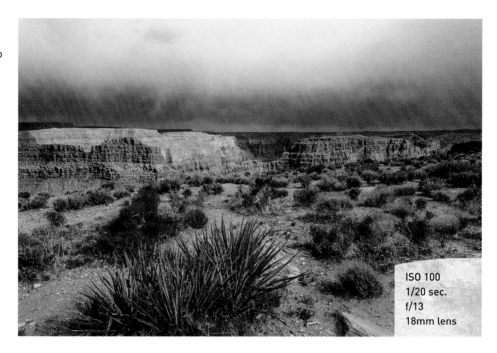

ISO 100
1/20 sec.
f/13
18mm lens

FIGURE 9.13
In this image of Valley of Fire State Park, emphasis is given to the sky by giving it the top two-thirds of the frame.

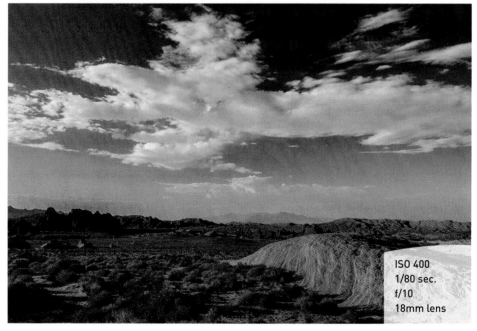

ISO 400
1/80 sec.
f/10
18mm lens

Chapter 9 Assignments

If you apply the shooting techniques and tools that you have learned in the previous chapters to these assignments, you'll improve your ability to incorporate good composition into your photos. Make sure you experiment with all the different elements of composition and see how you can combine them to add interest to your images.

Learning to see lines and patterns

Take your camera for a walk around your neighborhood and look for patterns and angles. Don't worry as much about getting great shots as developing an eye for details.

The ABCs of composition

Here's a great exercise that was given to me by my friend Vincent Versace: shoot the alphabet. This will be a little more difficult, but with practice you will start to see beyond the obvious. Don't just find letters in street signs and the like—instead, find objects that aren't really letters but that have the shape of letters.

Finding the square peg and the round hole

Circles, squares, and triangles. Spend a few sessions concentrating on shooting simple geometric shapes.

Using the aperture to focus attention

Depth of field plays an important role in defining your images and establishing depth and dimension. Practice shooting wide open, using your largest aperture for the narrowest depth of field. Then find a scene that would benefit from extended depth of field, using very small apertures to give sharpness throughout the scene.

Leading them into a frame

Look for scenes where you can use elements as leading lines, and then look for framing elements that you can use to isolate your subject and add both depth and dimension to your images.

Share your results with the book's Flickr group!

Join the group here: flickr.com/groups/t4i650dfromsnapshotstogreatshots

10

ISO 400
1/2000 sec.
f/2.8
70mm lens

Advanced Techniques

IMPRESS YOUR FAMILY AND FRIENDS

We covered a lot of ground in the previous chapters, especially on the general photographic concepts that apply to most, if not all, shooting situations. There are, however, some specific tools and techniques that will give you an added advantage in obtaining a great shot. Additionally, we will look at how to customize certain controls on your camera to reflect your personal shooting preferences and always have them at the ready.

PORING OVER THE PICTURE

I love leading photowalks for my fellow photographers. They are a great way of getting to know people who enjoy the same hobby, and they can be a learning environment as well. As a walk leader I am often asked how to shoot various scenarios, and on this photowalk in Orlando, Florida, one of the participants asked how to get a better sunset photo. It's really not all that hard once you know where to point your camera.

After locking in the exposure, I recomposed my image using the rule of thirds.

The Shady white balance setting added some warmth to the image.

Sunset shots look much better when you have some clouds in the sky.

Taking a meter reading on the brightest part of the sky helped to underexpose the image.

ISO 200
1/400 sec.
f/11
18mm lens

SPOT METER FOR MORE EXPOSURE CONTROL

Generally speaking, Evaluative metering mode provides accurate metering information for the majority of your photography. It does an excellent job of evaluating the scene and then relaying the proper exposure information to you. The only problem with this mode is that, like any metering mode on the camera, it doesn't know what it is looking at. There will be circumstances where you want to get an accurate reading from just a portion of a scene and discount the remaining area. To give you greater control of the metering operation, you can switch the camera to Spot metering mode. This allows you to take a meter reading from a very small circle in the center of the viewfinder, while ignoring the rest of the viewfinder area.

So when would you need to use this? Think of a person standing in front of a very dark wall. In Evaluative metering mode, the camera would see the entire scene and try to adjust the exposure information so that the dark background is exposed to render a lighter wall in your image. This means that the scene would actually be overexposed and your subject would then appear too light. To correct this, you can place the camera in Spot metering mode and take a meter reading right off of—and only off of—your subject, ignoring the dark wall altogether.

Other situations that would benefit from Spot metering include:

- Snow or beach environments where the overall brightness level of the scene could fool the meter

- Strongly backlit subjects that are leaving the subject underexposed

- Cases where the overall feel of a photo is too light or too dark (**Figures 10.1** and **10.2**)

SETTING UP AND SHOOTING IN SPOT METERING MODE

1. Press the Q button to bring up the Quick Control screen on the back of the camera, and then use the Cross keys to move the icon to the Metering mode.

2. Rotate the Main dial until the Spot metering icon appears, and then press the shutter release button halfway to return to shooting mode.

3. Point the center focus point at the subject that you wish to use for the meter reading.

4. Press the ✱ button to enable the AE Lock, which will hold the exposure value while you recompose, and then take the photo.

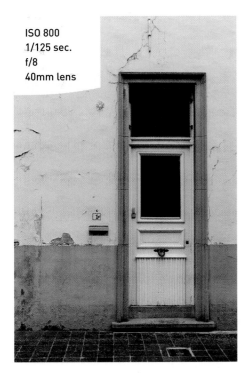

ISO 800
1/125 sec.
f/8
40mm lens

FIGURE 10.1
I was trying to get a good exposure of the door-way, but the light-colored wall was fooling the meter into underexposing.

ISO 800
1/60 sec.
f/8
40mm lens

FIGURE 10.2
By switching to Spot metering and measuring the doorframe, I was able to get a more accurate exposure.

When using Spot metering mode, remember that the meter believes it is looking at a medium gray value, so you might need to incorporate some exposure compensation of your own to the reading that you are getting from your subject. This will come from experience as you use the meter.

METERING FOR SUNRISE OR SUNSET

Capturing a beautiful sunrise or sunset is all about the sky. If there is too much foreground in the viewfinder, the camera's meter will deliver an exposure setting that is accurate for the darker foreground areas but leaves the sky looking overexposed, undersaturated, and generally just not very interesting (**Figure 10.3**). To gain more emphasis on the colorful sky, point your camera at the brightest part of it and take your meter reading there. Use the AE Lock and then recompose. The result will be an exposure setting that underexposes the foreground but provides a darker, more dramatic sky (**Figure 10.4**).

FIGURE 10.3
By metering with all the information in the frame, you get bright skies and more detail in the foreground.

ISO 200
1/30 sec.
f/11
30mm lens

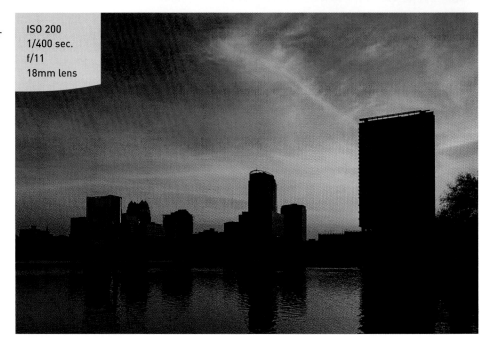

FIGURE 10.4
By taking the meter reading from the brightest part of the sky, you will get darker, more colorful sunsets.

ISO 200
1/400 sec.
f/11
18mm lens

MANUAL MODE

Probably one of the most advanced and yet most basic skills to master is shooting in Manual mode. With the power and utility of most of the automatic modes, Manual mode almost never sees the light of day. I have to admit that I don't select it for use very often, but there are times when no other mode will do. One situation that works well with Manual is studio work with external flashes. I know that when I work with studio lights, my exposure will not change, so I use Manual to eliminate any automatic changes that might happen from shooting in P, Tv, or Av mode.

Since you probably aren't too concerned with studio strobes at this point, I will concentrate on one of the ways in which you will want to use Manual mode for your photography: long nighttime exposures.

BULB PHOTOGRAPHY

If you want to work with long shutter speeds that don't quite fit into one of the selectable shutter speeds, you can select Bulb. This setting is available only in Manual mode, and its sole purpose is to open the shutter at your command and then close it again when you decide. I can think of two scenarios where this would come in handy: shooting fireworks and shooting lightning.

If you are photographing fireworks, you could certainly use one of the longer shutter speeds available in Tv mode, since they are available for exposure times up to 30 seconds. That is fine, but sometimes you don't need 30 seconds' worth of exposure and sometimes you need more.

BULB

If you are new to the world of photography, you might be wondering where in the world the *bulb* shutter function got its name. After all, wouldn't it make more sense to call it the Manual Shutter setting? It probably would, but this is one of those terms that harkens back to the origins of photography. Way back when, the shutter was actually opened through the use of a bulb-shaped device that forced air through a tube, which, in turn, pushed a plunger down, activating the camera shutter. When the bulb was released, it pulled the plunger back, letting the shutter close and ending the exposure.

If you open the shutter and then see a great burst of fireworks, you might decide that that is all you want for that particular frame, so you click the button to end the exposure (**Figure 10.5**). Set the camera to 30 seconds and you might get too many bursts, but if you shorten it to 10 seconds you might not get the one you want.

FIGURE 10.5
A great use for the bulb setting is capturing fireworks.

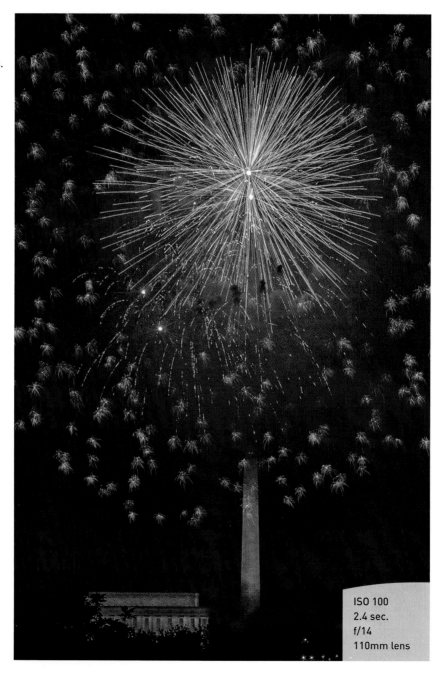

ISO 100
2.4 sec.
f/14
110mm lens

The same can be said for photographing a lightning storm. I have a friend who loves electrical storms, and he has some amazing shots that he captured using the Bulb setting. Lightning can be very tricky to capture, and using the Bulb setting to open and then close the shutter at will allows for more creativity, as well as more opportunity to get the shot.

To select the Bulb setting, simply place your camera in Manual mode and then rotate the Main dial until the shutter speed displays Bulb.

If you want to make a change to the aperture, hold in the Av button on the back of the camera while turning the Main dial.

When you're using the Bulb setting, the shutter will stay open only for the duration that you are holding down the shutter button. You will also see a counter on the lower-right portion of the LCD screen that will count off the seconds that the shutter is open. You can use this counter to either add or subtract time for your next shot. You should also be using a sturdy tripod or shooting surface to eliminate any self-induced vibration. The Bulb setting can be used in conjunction with the Mirror Lockup feature found in the Custom Setup menu for improved image sharpness.

I want to point out that using your finger on the shutter button for a bulb exposure will definitely increase the chances of getting some camera shake in your images. To get the most benefit from the Bulb setting, I suggest using a remote cord such as the Canon RS-60E3 Remote Switch (see the bonus chapter "Pimp My Ride" for more details). You'll also want to turn on the Long Exposure Noise Reduction, as covered in Chapter 7.

SHOOTING LIGHTNING

If you are going to photograph lightning strikes in a thunderstorm, please exercise extreme caution. Standing in the open with a tripod is like standing over a lightning rod. Work from indoors if at all possible.

AVOIDING LENS FLARE

Lens flare is one of the problems you will encounter when shooting in the bright sun. Lens flare will show itself as bright circles on the image (**Figure 10.6**). Often you will see multiple circles in a line leading from a very bright light source such as the sun. The flare is a result of the sun bouncing off the multiple pieces of optical glass in the lens and then being reflected back onto the sensor. Lens flare is especially frequent when using wide-angle lenses, because of their greater angle of coverage. You can avoid the problem using one of these methods:

- Try to shoot with the sun coming from over your shoulder, not in front of you or in your scene.

- Use a lens shade to block the unwanted light from striking the lens. You don't have to have the sun in your viewfinder for lens flare to be an issue. All it has to do is strike the front glass of the lens to make it happen.

- If you don't have a lens shade, just try using your hand or some other element to block the light.

FIGURE 10.6
The bright sun in the upper portion of the frame has created flare spots that are visible as colored circles radiating down through the image.

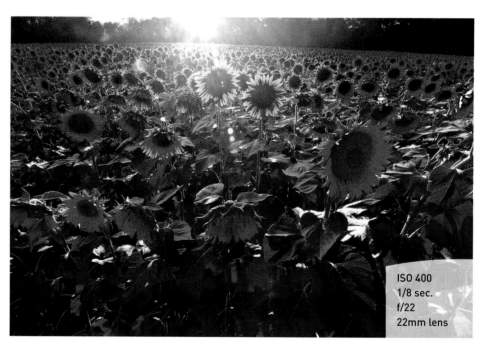

ISO 400
1/8 sec.
f/22
22mm lens

USING THE SUN CREATIVELY

Have you ever seen photographs where the sun is peeking through a small hole and it creates a very cool starburst effect (**Figure 10.7**)? There is actually a little trick to pulling it off, and it's fairly easy once you know how. The real key is to be shooting at f/22 (or whatever your smallest aperture is). Then you need to have just a small bit of the sunlight in your frame, either peeking over an edge or through a small hole. The other thing you need to do is make sure that you are properly exposing for the rest of your scene, not the bright bit of sunlight that you are allowing in. With a little practice, you can really make some very cool shots.

ISO 400
1/25 sec.
f/22
17mm lens

FIGURE 10.7
By letting the sun peek into my shot and using f/22, I was able to capture this cool starburst.

BRACKETING EXPOSURES

So what if you are doing everything right in terms of metering and mode selection, yet your images still sometimes come out too light or too dark? You can use a technique called *bracketing*, which will help you find the best exposure value for your scene by taking a normal exposure as well as ones that are over- and underexposed. Having these differing exposure values will most often present you with one frame that just looks better than the others. I use bracketing all the time.

Once you have entered the compensation/bracketing screen, you must use the Main dial to decide how much variation you want between bracketed exposures. You can set the amount of exposure bracketing from as little as a third of a stop to as much as two stops per exposure (this is the setting I use for creating HDR images). You can also dial in the amount of exposure compensation that you might need. You can adjust the compensation as much as seven stops in either direction, depending on the range of your bracketed exposures. Either way, bracketing will help you zero in on that perfect exposure, and you can just delete the ones that didn't make the grade (**Figures 10.8** through **10.10**).

You can adjust the Exposure Compensation/AEB setting through the camera menu or by using my favorite method, the Quick Control screen.

FIGURE 10.8
One stop of exposure below normal.

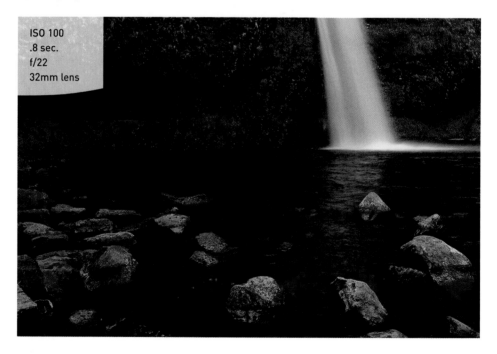

ISO 100
.8 sec.
f/22
32mm lens

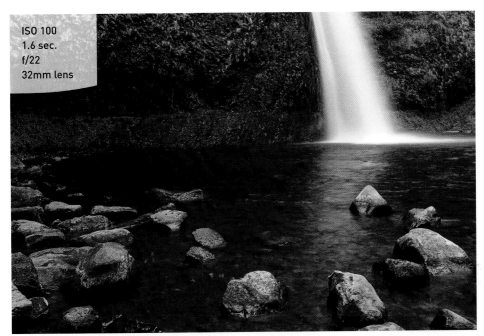

ISO 100
1.6 sec.
f/22
32mm lens

FIGURE 10.9
The normal exposure as indicated by the camera meter.

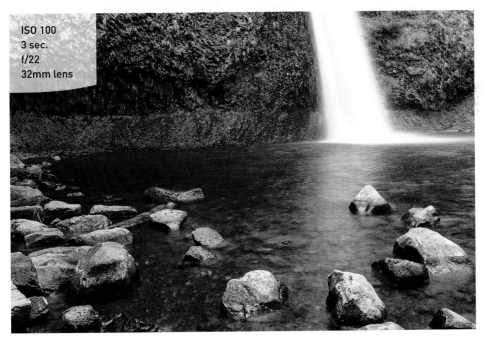

ISO 100
3 sec.
f/22
32mm lens

FIGURE 10.10
One stop of exposure above normal.

SETTING AUTO-EXPOSURE BRACKETING

1. Press the Q button and then move the cursor to the Exposure Compensation/AEB setting icon (**A**).

2. Press Set to enter the compensation/bracketing screen (**B**).

3. Use the Main dial to set the amount of over- and underexposure that you desire (**C**).

4. If you want the "normal" exposure to be a little over- or underexposed, you can adjust that with your left/right Cross keys.

The camera will take the underexposed image first, then the normal image, then the overexposed image. Don't forget to take all three.

When I am out shooting, I typically shoot with my camera set to an exposure compensation of –1/3 stop to protect my highlights. If I am dealing with a subject that has a lot of different tonal ranges from bright to dark, I will often bracket by one stop over and one stop under my already compensated exposure. That means I will have exposures of –1 1/3, –1/3, and +2/3.

The Auto Exposure Bracketing feature will reset itself when the camera is turned off and then on again.

HDR BACKLIGHT CONTROL

Earlier in the book I explained the process for creating HDR images using three separate images that need to be combined using special software. There is, however, a special feature on your camera that will let you take three images and combine them right in your camera for improved highlight and shadow details. It's called HDR Backlight Control, and you can activate it by selecting it on the Mode dial. It lives on the Basic zone side of the dial because you really have no ability to change its options.

When you select the HDR Backlight Control option, the camera will take three continuous photos with a single click of the shutter button. After the photos have been taken, the camera will combine the images to give you an image with greater detail in the highlights and shadows (**Figure 10.11**).

There are limitations to using this setting. First, you should always have your camera on a stable surface or a tripod when taking photos. Second, you should only use it on non-moving subjects, because you can get ghosting if there is movement during the exposure process.

ISO 2000
1/160 sec.
f/3.5
18mm lens

FIGURE 10.11
There is a great deal of detail in both the shadows and the highlights of the backlit subject thanks to the HDR processing.

AUTO LIGHTING OPTIMIZER

Did you know that your camera provides a function that can automatically make your pictures look better? It's called Auto Lighting Optimizer. It works this way: the camera evaluates the tones in your image and then lightens any areas that it believes are too dark or lacking in contrast (**Figures 10.12** and **10.13**). This is different than the HDR Backlight Control because it is working on only a single exposure and boosting the shadows while pulling the exposure down slightly to darken the highlights. This optimization is applied automatically in the shooting modes of the Basic zone.

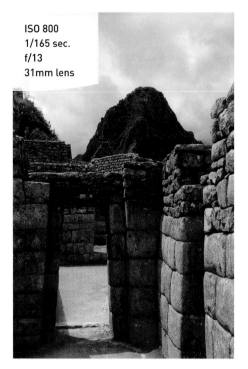

ISO 800
1/165 sec.
f/13
31mm lens

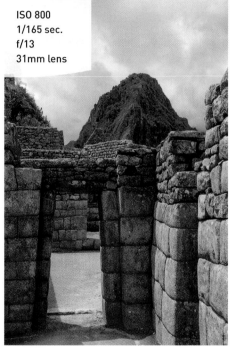

ISO 800
1/165 sec.
f/13
31mm lens

FIGURE 10.12
Without the Auto Lighting Optimizer, the shadows are dark and contrasty.

FIGURE 10.13
Although the exposure hasn't changed, the shadows are brighter after changing the Optimizer to the High setting.

You can choose from four levels: Disable, Low, Standard, and High. You will need to evaluate the strength of the effect on your images and change it accordingly. I typically leave it set to Standard so that I have brighter, more detailed shadow areas in my photographs. If you are using exposure compensation to darken your image, you might find that your image is too bright with this option turned on. Also, you should disable it if you are using flash exposure compensation since it will try to work against you when you alter the flash strength.

SETTING UP THE AUTO LIGHTING OPTIMIZER

1. Press the Menu button, use the Main dial to get to the second setup tab, highlight Auto Lighting Optimizer, and press the Set button (**A**).

2. Use the Cross keys to select the level of optimization that you prefer, and press the Set button to lock in the change (**B**).

B

Auto Lighting Optimizer
Standard

INFO. ✓ Disable during man expo

SET OK

HANDHELD NIGHT SCENE

Another great little automatic feature in the T4i is the Handheld Night Scene mode. This is yet another Basic shooting mode, and it acts in a similar fashion to the HDR mode except it is made for getting a sharp image in low-light or night scenes, where handholding a camera usually isn't possible. To do this, the camera fires off four continuous frames and then processes them in-camera to create one sharp, properly exposed image (**Figure 10.14**). You even have the option of combining the mode with flash if you want to include someone in the photo. Just make sure that you turn the flash on using the Q button, and have the person stand fairly still during the picture.

ISO 800
1/40 sec.
f/3.5
18mm lens

FIGURE 10.14
Handheld Night Scene combines your photos to give you one sharp, noise-free image.

THE MY MENU SETTING

There are a lot of items in the menu that you can change, but some are used and changed more frequently than others. The My Menu function allows you to place six of your most-used menu items in one place so that you can quickly get to them, make your changes, and get on with shooting. You can see what I have in my My Menu in **Figure 10.15**.

FIGURE 10.15
Here are the six functions I have stored in the My Menu function.

CUSTOMIZING YOUR MY MENU SETTING

1. Press the Menu button, and use the Cross keys to select the tab with the star.

2. Select My Menu settings, and press Set (**A**).

3. Highlight Register to My Menu, and press Set (**B**).

4. Scroll through the available menu items, and when you highlight one that you want to add, press the Set button (**C**).

5. When asked if you want to register the item, highlight OK and press Set (**D**).

6. Continue adding the items that you want in the list until you have selected your favorites (up to six of them).

7. You can sort your menu items as you see fit, or if you change your mind, you can delete them individually or all at once. It's all up to you.

CUSTOMIZE YOUR WHITE BALANCE

Previous chapters have addressed the issue of setting your white balance, but what if you are in a situation that doesn't fall neatly into one of the existing categories like Daylight or Tungsten? You might want to consider creating a custom white balance. This is especially helpful if you have more than one kind of light source shining on your subject. A perfect example might be indoors with fluorescent lighting fixtures overhead and daylight coming through a window. To ensure that you are getting the best-possible results in a situation like this, you can perform a quick white balance customization by using the Custom White Balance option. Don't worry, though—it's easier than you might think. Typically, the only thing you will need is a piece of white paper.

CREATING A CUSTOM WHITE BALANCE

1. Begin by having your subject hold a piece of white paper, and then take a picture of it. You can have the camera set on any white balance preset for this (**A**).

2. Next, press the Menu button, navigate to the second shooting menu, highlight Custom White Balance, and press the Set button (**B**).

3. The camera should then display the photo that you took of the white paper. If it is the correct image, press the Set button. If it is not, use the left/right Cross keys to locate the image first (**C**).

4. Confirm that this is the image that you want to use by highlighting the OK option and pressing Set (**D**).

5. Click OK to set your camera to the Custom White Balance setting (**E**).

You are now ready to take images with much more accurate color for the environment where you are shooting.

CONCLUSION

As you'll see, the online bonus chapter "Pimp My Ride" covers a lot of gadgets, filters, and accessories that will make your photography better. It can become an obsession to always have the latest thing out there. But here's the deal. You already have almost everything you need to take great pictures: an awesome camera and the knowledge necessary to use it. Everything else is just icing on the cake. So, although I introduce a few items in "Pimp My Ride" that I do think will make your photographic life easier and even improve your images, don't get caught up in the technology and gadgetry.

Use your knowledge of basic photography to explore everything your camera has to offer. Explore the limits of your camera. Don't be afraid to take bad pictures. Don't be too quick to delete them from your memory card, either. Take some time to really look at them and see where things went wrong. Look at your camera settings and see if perhaps there was a change you could have made to make things better. Be your toughest critic and learn from your mistakes. With practice and reflection, you will soon find your photography getting better and better. Not only that, but your instincts will improve to the point that you will come upon a scene and know exactly how you want to shoot it before you even take your camera out of the bag.

Chapter 10 Assignments

Many of the techniques covered in this chapter are specific to certain shooting situations that may not come about very often. This is even more reason to practice them so that when the situation does present itself you will be ready.

Adding some drama to the end of the day

Most sunset photos don't reflect what the photographer saw, because they weren't metered correctly. The next time you see a colorful sunset, pull out your camera and take a meter reading from the sky, and take a photo. Then take a photo without a meter reading, and see what a difference it makes.

Making your exposure spot-on

Using the Spot metering mode can give accurate results, but only when the camera is pointed at something that has a middle tone. Try adding something gray to the scene and taking a reading off it. Now switch back to your regular metering mode and see if the exposure isn't slightly different.

Using the Bulb setting to capture the moment

This is definitely one of those settings that you won't use often, but it's pretty handy when you need it. If you have the opportunity to shoot a fireworks display or a distant storm, try setting the camera to Bulb and then playing with some long exposures to capture just the moments that you want.

Bracketing your way to better exposures

Why settle for just one variation of an image when you can bracket to get the best exposure choice? Set your camera up for a 1/3-stop bracket series, and then expand it to a one-stop series. Review the results to see if the normal setting was the best or perhaps one of the bracketed exposures was even better.

Share your results with the book's Flickr group!

Join the group here: flickr.com/groups/t4i650dfromsnapshotstogreatshots

INDEX